Coordinating geography across the primary school

THE SUBJECT LEADER'S HANDBOOKS

Series Editor: Mike Harrison, Centre for Primary Education, School of Education, The University of Manchester, Oxford Road, Manchester, M13 9DP

Coordinating geography across the primary school

John Halocha

FALMER PRESS

Taylor & Francis Group

| UK | The Falmer Press, 1 Gunpowder Square, London, EC4A 3DE |
| USA | The Falmer Press, Taylor & Francis Inc., 1900 Frost Road, Suite 101, Bristol, PA 19007 |

© J. Halocha, 1998

First published in 1998

A catalogue record for this book is available from the British Library

ISBN 0 7507 0692 9 paper

Library of Congress Cataloging-in-Publication Data are available on request

Jacket design by Carla Turchini

Typeset in 10/14pt Melior and printed by Graphicraft Typesetters Ltd., Hong Kong

Contents

Part three
Whole school policies and schemes of work

Part four
Monitoring for quality

Part five
Resources for learning

Series editor's preface

This book has been prepared for primary teachers charged with the responsibility of acting as the geography coordinator for their school. It forms part of a series of new publications that set out to advise such teachers on the complex issues of improving teaching and learning through managing each element of the primary school curriculum.

Why is there a need for such a series? Most authorities recognise, after all, that the quality of the primary children's work and learning depends upon the skills of their class teacher, not in the structure of management systems, policy documents or the titles and job descriptions of staff. Many today recognise that school improvement equates directly to the improvement of teaching so surely all tasks, other than imparting subject knowlege, are merely a distraction for the committed primary teacher.

Nothing should take teachers away from their most important role, that is, serving the best interests of the class of children in their care and this book and the others in the series does not wish to diminish that mission. However, the increasing complexity of the primary curriculum and society's expanding expectations, makes it very difficult for the class teacher to keep up to date with every development. Within traditional subject areas there has been an explosion of knowledge and new fields introduced such as science, technology, design, problem solving and health education, not to mention the uses of computers. These are now considered entitlements for primary children. Furthermore, we now expect all children to succeed at these studies, not just the fortunate few. All this has overwhelmed a class teacher system largely unchanged since the inception of primary schools.

Primary class teachers cannot possibly be an expert in every aspect of the curriculum they are required to teach. To whom can they turn for help? It is unrealistic to assume that such support will be available from the headteacher whose responsibilities have grown ever wider since the 1988 Educational Reform Act. Constraints, including additional staff costs, and the loss of benefits from the strength and security of the class teacher system, militate against wholesale adoption of specialist or semi-specialist teaching. Help therefore has to come from exploiting the talents of teachers themselves, in a process of mutual support. Hence primary schools have chosen many and varied systems of consultancy or subject coordination which best suit the needs of their children and the current expertise of the staff.

In fact, curriculum leadership functions in primary schools have increasingly been shared with class teachers through the policy of curriculum coordination for the past twenty years, especially to improve the consistency of work in language and mathematics. Since then each school has developed their own system and the series recognises that the one each reader is part of will be a compromise between the ideal and the possible. Campbell and Neill (1994) show that by 1991 nearly nine out of every ten primary class teachers had such responsibility and the average number of subjects each was between 1.5 and 2.2 (depending on the size of school).

These are the people for whom this series sets out to help to do this part of their work. The books each deal with specific issues whilst at the same time providing an overview of general themes in the management of the subject curriculum. The term *subject leader* is used in an inclusive sense and combines the two major roles that such teachers play when they have responsibility for subjects and aspects of the primary curriculum.

The books each deal with:
coordination; a role which emphasises harmonising, bringing together, making links, establishing routines and common practice; and
subject leadership — a role which emphasises providing information, offering expertise and direction, guiding the development of the subject, and raising standards.

The purpose of the series is to give practical guidance and support to teachers, in particular what to do and how to do it. They each offer help on the production, development and review of policies and schemes of work; the organization of resources, and developing strategies for improving the management of the subject curriculum.

Each book in the series contains material that subject managers will welcome and find useful in developing their subject expertise and in tackling problems of enthusing and motivating staff.

Each book has five parts.
1 The review and development of the different roles coordinators are asked to play.
2 Updating subject knowledge and subject pedagogical knowledge.
3 Developing and maintaining policies and schemes of work.
4 Monitoring work within the school to enhance the continuity of teaching and progression in pupil's learning.
5 Resources and contacts.

Although written primarily for teachers who are geography coordinators, John Halocha's book offers practical guidance and many insights for anyone in the school who has a responsibility for the geography curriculum, including teachers with an overall role in coordinating the whole or key stage curriculum and the deputy head and headteacher.

The book is easily readable and offers many practical hints and useful advice. It will help readers attempting to develop a whole-school view of progress in geography particularly those who are new to the job or have recently changed schools. This book will help readers to develop both the subject expertise they will need and the managerial perspective necessary to enthuse and inform others.

Mike Harrison, Series Editor
January 1998

Acknowledgments

The author wishes to thank Carole Goodchild, headteacher of Newtown Infant School, Stockton on Tees for her advice and permission to reproduce school policy documents.

Grateful thanks also to colleagues in the School of Education, University of Durham for all their support during the writing of this book.

Part one

The role of the geography coordinator

Chapter 1
Contexts for effective coordination

Chapter 2
Developing your skill as geography coordinator

Chapter 3
Establishing a secure place for geography in the school curriculum

Contexts for effective coordination

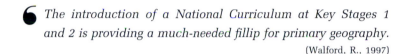

The introduction of a National Curriculum at Key Stages 1 and 2 is providing a much-needed fillip for primary geography.
(Walford, R., 1997)

Introduction

Children have experienced a great deal of relevant and interesting geography since the introduction of the 1991 Orders. Many primary school teachers have worked hard to implement these requirements and the Dearing revisions. This is a very different situation from that described by HMI in 1989 when they wrote that 'overall standards of work in geography were very disappointing' DES (1989). The role of the classteacher has been crucial and remains at the centre of British primary education. Teachers are concerned with the development of the whole child, the provision of secure relationships and the creation of a supportive and effective learning environment.

Although the class teacher remains central in primary education, the complex nature of both the management of schools and the curriculum itself means that teachers are unable to keep fully informed about developments in all subjects. The increasing accountability of schools demands that they have some way of ensuring that each subject is carefully planned and pupil progess is monitored. This role is increasingly becoming the responsibility of the subject manager. The purpose of this book to allows for a discussion of the role of the geography curriculum manager in the primary school and it is expected that it will be read by these members of staff and other members of the school community with management responsibilities for deploying curriculum leaders effectively, such as headteachers, governors and others.

Your position as geography curriculum manager will not have come about by chance. It is the result of a number of decisions taken in your school and is part of the ongoing changes taking place in the institution and within the wider world of education. This chapter will discuss the context of your role and hopefully clarify why your school needs you as a geography coordinator. It should encourage you to look closely to see how your work relates to the whole school community and perhaps begin to ask some key questions to help clarify your role and the aims you hope to develop. It accepts that every school will be different and that you also come to your role in various ways: you may be a newly appointed member of staff who is busy finding out about the culture of your school. You may be an established team member who has been asked to take geography as a new responsibility. Perhaps you have a geography qualification, if so you will be a rare breed in the world of primary education! You may feel confident and enthusiastic about your role, but you may also have concerns which 'may result in a temporary questioning of ability and suitability for leadership, throwing up all manner of doubts and insecurities.' Day et al. (1993). The rest of this book aims to build on your expertise and help you infect your colleagues with a real enthusiasm to develop their teaching of primary geography.

The broader context

In 1992 Alexander, Rose and Woodhead's report *Curriculum Organisation and Classroom Practice in Primary Schools* discussed four roles which primary teachers might adopt in

> Geography in the National Curriculum is silent on the overall aims of geographical education, though clearly these can be inferred from the Programmes of Study [but they] do not explain why these objectives are worth pursuing   (Graves, 1997)

managing subjects. You might like to consider which of these models are at work in your school and the subjects where they are in operation. What are the advantages and problems with each approach? What can you learn from this in negotiating the role you feel will be most effective for primary geography? Might your role include a number of these at various times?

- **The generalist** teaches most or all of the curriculum, probably specialising in an age-range rather than a subject and does not profess specialist knowledge for consultancy.
- **The generalist/consultant** combines a generalist role in part of the curriculum with cross-school coordination, advice and support in one or more subjects.
- **The semi-specialist** teaches his or her subject, but also has a generalist or consultancy role.
- **The specialist** teaches his or her subject full time (as in the case of music in some primary schools).

(Alexander, Rose and Woodhead, 1992: para 146)

Later papers (OFSTED, 1994) refined definitions of the role of generalist/consultant teachers and your school will have based its decisions on how to interpret these on a number of factors. A large school may be able to afford the luxury of each teacher being responsible for one subject area, whereas in a small school a teacher may manage two or three subjects. You are going to have to work within this framework and make practical decisions about what can be realistically done and when in order to ensure success and development. Research by Webb (1994) shows that 'the amount and nature of the work fulfilled by coordinators varied enormously from school to school, and often between coordinators in the same school'. It is worth bearing this in mind when talking with other geography coordinators and attending various course. Look out for examples of good practice within a broader context, but always adapt them to the needs of your own school.

Throughout this book we shall be looking at ways of developing, managing and monitoring an effective primary geography curriculum, but underpinning this is the fact that 'The National Curriculum has not yet provided us with a philosophy for primary geography', (Morgan, 1994).

It is perhaps reassuring that with so much central control of education, these important aspects of geographical education have been left for the professionals to define. It is certainly something which needs to appear in your geography policy, which in turn may be seen in action in the school. Within this broader context, you need to begin to develop your ideas about why geography is important and the aims of the curriculum you will develop alongside other teachers. Also, begin to think about how you can find out what your colleagues believe geography to be about and then think about how these may provide the foundation of a geography policy owned by all members of staff. The Orders have given us this opportunity and it is important that, as professionals, we take it up and use it within the context of our own schools. This is especially important for geography as much of our work starts in the locality of the school and from children's developing understanding of the world around them.

Unlike some subjects, for example history, the factual content within the geography Orders is quite small. Again, this is an excellent opportunity for each school to interpret the requirements in its own context. It's also one of the challenges you will have to meet in curriculum planning and building effective schemes of work based on the broad building blocks of skills, places and themes. The geography Orders also offer many opportunities for you to interpret words and phrases flexibly in order to build an exciting and relevant set of learning experiences, for example, at Key Stage 2 when working on Thematic Studies 'Contexts should include the United Kingdom and the European Union'. (DfE, 1995). Many schools have focused in on the words 'European Union' and developed excellent studies and links with other EU schools. One of the interesting parts of your work will be seeing how the Orders may be adapted to the needs of your children in school. The school will already be using some ideas about what a relevant geography content actually is. 'Each teacher, however, may also have his or her agenda according to the circumstances in which he or she is teaching'. (Graves, 1997). Your role will be to begin to understand these interpretations and bring them together into a coherent set of experiences for your children.

Within the broad context of education, your curriculum area is one not requiring End-of-Key Stage Assessments. Indeed, for 1998 and beyond 'there are no plans to introduce statutory teacher assessment in Key Stages 1 and 2' (SCAA, 1997c) in geography. Think about this position from the point of view of the core subjects. Teachers have to spend a great deal of time preparing for, conducting and following up the results of statutory tests over which they have very little control or influence, in mathematics, English and science. They are also highly public and political. In contrast, you and your colleagues have almost total control over how you assess children's developing geographical knowledge, skills and understanding. Marsden (1994) identifies a number of advantages in this situation:

- teachers have more flexibility in devising their own appraisals;
- opportunities exist to harness a wide range of assessment instruments;
- assessment can be an integral part of the curriculum planning process.

Hopefully, you are encourged by the benefits created in this situation and will perhaps be able to work with colleagues on ways of making the most of the opportunity for professional, school-based development of geographical assessment.

The final major feature of the broader context of your work is inspection. At some time OFSTED will visit your school. You will have an important role to play in this process. The key to success is being well informed on all the key issues relating to geography. We have talked about the Orders and assessment requirement imposed from beyond the school; inspectors will also focus in on what is actually happening in your school. They take into account the location of your establishment. All the main features of the school will be studied: policies, staffing, resources, budgets, pupil behaviour, views of parents, planning papers etc. As a curriculum manager you will need to understand what is happening in your school and how all these things affect your work in geography. The next section discusses the key areas.

Your school context

We have briefly looked at the main frameworks which are imposed on the school from outside. This section will focus in on what may be happening in your school context and how they affect your work as a curriculum manager.

When you take on the role of geography coordinator you are taking a particular place within a team. A great many processes will be at work within this team. Some of them you will be able to influence and others you will have to accept it is not possible to change. Each school is very different: if you have moved to your post from another school, assume that very little will be the same. Indeed, in an era of central control this is a reassuring feature of English primary education. The most effective coordinators do a lot of looking, listening and asking questions. Begin to get to know your school context. Even if you have taken on the role from within the school, some things may have changed. If you now have a promoted post for your work, how might this affect other colleagues' views about you? Does this give you power and status or do you in fact have to work even harder alongside other staff?

Teams work in many different ways. Belbin's (1981) work on successful teams showed the need for teams to contain people with specific skills, knowledge, aptitudes, interests and personalities which could be interlocked to form an effective working relationship. The head and governors have a key role to play here in appointing staff but many staff are inherited and it may be hard to change attitudes. Think about the following questions in relation to the team with whom you will be working.

■ What does my personality contribute to the team? How does it complement other team members? (Your knowledge of the school may be helpful here: the last coordinator may have been unwilling to support other staff and just saw their role as a resource provider. How can you use your personality to promote the development of geography?)

■ What skills might assist other team members? What can I learn from the skills other people have? (For example, if you admit to not being an IT expert, how might you develop a relationship with the IT coordinator to both improve your IT skills and begin to integrate IT within the geography curriculum?)

- What knowledge do I bring to the team? (You may have a geography qualification which has given you clear subject knowledge others may like to share.)
- Can I use my aptitude for designing learning resources?
- What interests do I have to support my work? (You may be a keen supporter of environmental issues. Your contacts and knowledge could enrich the work done and indeed required at both Key Stages 1 and 2.)

This final example was chosen to highlight the need for some caution. Your own values and burning interests can rub off on staff and children to good effect, but it will be your job to maintain a balance and lack of bias in the curriculum. 'Here one enters the realm of values. One of the most significant shifts to have occurred in the curriculum in the 1990s is the shift towards the instrumental aims of education' (Graves, 1997). Part of your work within the team may be to represent a subject providing opportunities for children to discuss values and controversial issues. This is also where your knowledge of the school culture and history will be important in order to assess what might be possible, what has happened before and what people thought about it. 'The first of your givens is the nature of your teacher colleagues. You have to work with them and appreciate that however enthusiastic you are about your proposals, coordination, like politics, is the art of the possible' (Harrison, 1995). This is what teamwork is about.

The management style within your school will have an effect on the type and quality of work you can achieve. Sometimes, if you have worked in a school for a period of time you begin to take the culture for granted. It's not easy to stand back to see how this culture might be affecting your work. A practical example for the geography coordinator might be the school policy on fieldwork. An accident a few years ago may have established a culture where fieldwork is not encouraged, so you need to know this background in order to begin some process of change. Headteachers, senior staff and governors need to be supportive of your work. Here are some questions you might think about in relation to how school management influences the coordinator's role.

■ Am I clear about what the headteacher expects me to do?

■ Have I discussed with her/him what I see my role to be and the stages of development?

■ Do I have information about the School Development Plan and budgets in order to see how I may build in my development work in geography?

■ What public support and encouragement am I realistically likely to receive from management?

■ How flexible is my job description to enable me to show enterprise and initiative?

■ What status does geography appear to have in the eyes of management?

The answers to these and similar questions will help you decide the ways in which you plan to influence change within the school from your position in the team.

Another area especially important for geography is its position within the whole curriculum. In a literal sense this may actually mean that you see it timetabled for a couple of afternoons in the summer term once SATs have been completed. Such evidence may give you some clues about the perceived status of the subject. But it can go deeper than this. 'Geography is not a core subject in the National Curriculum. It is perceived as being of minor importance by some teachers, and others, with no immediate commitment to the subject.' (Chambers and Donert, 1996). You will need to begin to understand how these attitudes work at various levels. At a whole school level it may have a considerable effect on your resourcing if the governor budget sub-committee always allocates the greatest funds to the core subjects. Incidentally, the Geographical Association publishes a leaflet for school governors and parents on the role of geography in the whole school curriculum. How are you going to develop a case for at least some more spending on geography? The status of the subject can also be assessed by its location and time allocation within the curriculum. Although SCAA provides information on how many hours are to be allocated to each subject, they are not followed in all schools. Geography can also be hidden within topics and this can result in a continuation of what HMI found in the 1980s when they reported that where it 'was taught through topic work . . . there was a tendency for geography to lose its distinctive contribution' (DES, 1989). How might you begin to work with other coordinators on developing the place of geography within the whole curriculum? Planning is a complex process and if a system has been established you will need to develop a clear case for change if you feel it is needed. Another influence on the position and status of geography is parental perception of the subject. Many parents understand the need for reading, writing and numeracy having a central place and major allocation of time in the primary school. Far fewer may have views on the value of geography. One of the skills you may need to develop is how a supportive and lively parental attitude towards geography can be established. Ways of achieving this will be discussed later in the book.

Most, if not all of your colleagues, will have to teach geography. To help them do this well, you will need to understand their backgrounds, levels of expertise and attitudes towards the subject. These questions are included to help you begin this process.

- Do they appear to value geography as a subject in the primary school?
- What have they actually been doing in geography recently?
- What messages do you think they pass on to the children about the subject?
- What skills, knowledge, contacts and enthusiasms do they have to support good geography teaching and learning?
- What positive experiences have they had which you can build on?
- What ideas do they have about how you can help lead the subject in your school?
- Can you identify key people to help you with your work?
- How do they currently teach, record and assess geography?
- What resources do they use and how confident are they in using them?

As you try to answer these questions, keep a record of the information and ideas you collect. This may help you begin to work out a plan for which jobs to tackle first and where to target your activities. For example, you may identify a colleague who is quietly doing a superb job in teaching geography, hidden away in their mobile classroom. If you can find ways of celebrating their good work, you may also start to develop a support group within the staff as a whole.

What geographical skills, understanding and knowledge do your pupils already possess? For example, how well can they use an atlas? Is geographical competence more apparent in certain age groups? Why? How do children talk about people living in other countries? Where have your children visited? 'All children have their own "little geographies", whether it be Carmen de la Legua in Lima or the Edge Hill district of Liverpool', (Chambers and Donert, 1996). How much of these do you understand? These and similar lines of enquiry can all help to build up a picture to inform decisions about the type of geographical experiences which will be relevant to the children. Fortunately, the structure and open-ended content of the Orders will allow you to do this: not every subject coordinator is as lucky.

The final, but very important aspect of the school context in which you are working is yourself. At the time you are reading this you will be at a specific point in your personal life and school career. What implications might these have for your role as a geography coordinator?

One area to consider is your own position within the school. The length of time you have been in the school and the level of post you hold will be viewed in various ways by other members of staff. Are there power groups with particular agendas of which you need to be aware because they view you and geography in a particular way? How can you build on the strengths of what you have already achieved in the school? Primary teachers are good at under-valuing their successes, so it is worth looking at what has already gone well and is respected within the school community.

What experiences and qualifications do you have which may be of use in your role? You may have forgotten the orienteering course you attended years ago and which may have provided many useful skills. If you have qualifications in geography, do not assume all the other members of staff know what you take for granted. For example, you may have a clear idea of the processes at work in a river, but it is very unlikely to be common knowledge amongst the staff. Don't be put off by your apparent lack of qualifications in geography if that is your situation. Enthusiasm and a keen interest in wanting to develop the subject will more than make up for them. At some point you may wish to gain a qualification, but using the ideas and sources of information and contacts described in this book will hopefully guide you down the road to becoming an informed geography coordinator before then.

Think also about your overall responsibilities and duties within the school. If you have more than one subject area and perhaps a whole school issue to manage, you will only be able to give so much time to geography. Time management and a plan of the order in which you will carry out your work will help you to achieve your aims. We will look at these issues in later chapters.

Finally, you may be the designated geography coordinator but you cannot do everything on your own. Try to begin to work out where help is available.

- If you are writing a policy, can the school secretary help with desktop publishing?
- How much notice does s/he need?
- Are you aware of the help available from local advisers and resource centres?
- Do you know what INSET provision there is in your area?
- How much has already been done in the school and where is it? For example, there may be a set of useful locality photos collecting dust in a cupboard.
- How much use is made of Geographical Association resources and events?
- What documents do you need to obtain to guide your decision-making?
- How might your pupils and the wider community help you develop a rich geographical education in your school?

We began this chapter thinking about the philosophy of geographical education. Morgan (1994) suggests that 'the philosophy for geography in the primary school will not be created by government Order, nor by the publishers of textbooks and resources. It will be created by teachers and children'. By taking on the role of geography coordinator you will be helping to create a philosophy about people and the world in which they live that will be relevant to both your pupils and their teachers.

Chapter 2 — Developing your skills as geography coordinator

> ❛ *By considering your actions carefully you can determine the most appropriate way to ensure progress.* (Harrison, 1995)

Becoming an effective geography coordinator

Your work as a coordinator will be strongly influenced by the contexts discussed in the previous chapter. However, perhaps one of the most important skills you can bring to your role is the ability to get on with people. If you are successful, there is a much greater possibility of change occurring, but change itself is an interesting feature within the school environment. It is unlikely to occur simply by presenting staff with a completed policy, a large pile of maps — or through the imposition of more government legislation. 'Change occurs only when teachers believe in the need for it, know where it is going, are committed to it and have some ownership of it,' (Harrison, 1995) are important points to bear in mind when you undertake your role of geography coordinator. Colleagues will be looking at how you develop your role and drawing inferences about what you actually believe in and intend to do.

We give other people clues about our beliefs and approaches to the job in various ways. Everard and Morris (1985) suggest a number of skills needed by curriculum coordinators that will promote change and development in their schools. The following list is adapted from their ideas. Consider it from three points of view: first, to what extent do you think you possess these skills? Second, how useful might they be in your school context? Finally, do you actually agree with them and what else might you add?

- to act consistently;
- to maintain hope, belief and optimism;
- to want success (although not necessarily public approval);
- to be willing to take calculated risks and accept the consequences;
- to develop a capacity to accept, deal with and use conflict constructively;
- to learn to use a soft voice and a low key manner;
- to develop self awareness;
- to cultivate a tolerance of ambiguity and complexity;
- to avoid viewing issues as simply black and white;
- to become an active listener.

adapted from Everard and Morris (1985)

When you have thought about the three questions, look again at the list and think of possible examples where they might fit directly into your work as geography coordinator. This is one example to start your thinking.

- *to be willing to take calculated risks and accept the consequences*

Your Year 5 teacher met an Italian headteacher on holiday who would like a link with an English school. S/he has a lot of contact details to get started. S/he has never really shown any strong interest in geography in the past but says s/he remembered a point you had discussed in the Themes section in the Orders where the study of a European context is encouraged.

What would you do? This is a practical example of the type of decision you will be making as a coordinator. It will involve a lot of work. The advantages for children's active learning, the development of resources and the profile of the subject could be great, but how serious are the Italian teachers? To what extent might you be able to involve this colleague in taking the initiative in the project? How can you justify it within the whole curriculum plan and indeed the school development plan?

This example illustrates a number of ways in which your ability to manage and build relationships are a crucial part of your work. Your immediate reaction to the suggestion will be watched very carefully. You must be ready to respond, yet finding the right level of enthusiasm and an understanding of the real implications of the suggestion will not be easy. This is where your knowledge of the background in which you work is important.

- How might the head respond and do you know his/her views about developing a European dimension in the curriculum?
- Have you already mentioned Europe in your medium term plans and set some seeds for progress?
- Might this be an excellent means of directly involving a member of staff and hence giving them considerable ownership of the work?
- How influential is this member of staff: might they then be able to bring others into more geographical work or could it inhibit your longer term plans?

Another source of information available to you is to observe how other subject coordinators manage their subjects and attempt to assess the response and change they actually achieve.

Using your skills to develop your role

This section will examine a range of practical activities that you will probably have to initiate in your role and we shall discuss the skills that may be helpful in achieving your goals. Each school will be at a different stage of development, so having looked at where you are, a set of small and achievable steps will need to be planned and taken, using some of these ideas and building in your own.

Find out what is going on in geography in your school

You may already know a lot about the broad context described in the first chapter, but now you need to focus in on geography. If you are able to collect some clear evidence you may have a stronger case for your ideas, which should also help you to prioritise what you want to do and where you think the most effective impact for change can take place. There are a variety of ways in which you could collect your information.

- **Looking and listening.** How is geography taught? Are there geographical displays anywhere?
- **Asking questions.** What parts of the geography curriculum have teachers enjoyed teaching? Do they know where resources are available? Talk to the children about geography and ask them about the local area.
- **Reading children's work, policy documents, teachers' plans, current schemes of work, LEA guidelines, OFSTED reports, minutes of governors' meetings.** All these will give you useful information to help review current policy and practice.

Know what the headteacher expects you to do

When you discuss this with her/him, be clear about your own ideas and begin to negotiate a plan of action.

- You will need to show your enthusiasm and commitment to advocate geography in the school and inspire other members of staff.
- How flexible and helpful is your job description?
- Can you begin to negotiate taking control of a small budget and gradually build this up?
- Demonstrate that you have thought about your role carefully.
- Aim to get the head on your side.

Begin to place geography within the school development plan

You are dependent on the workings of the school development cycle. You cannot suddenly expect resources to come your way, nor can major changes be made in the curriculum, which may, for example, be running on a two yearly cycle, but you can present your own staged plan and negotiate where and what needs to be built into this official document. Offer to attend a governors' meeting to discuss your ideas. These will probably include staff development, resources, curriculum plans and perhaps fieldwork policies. Once you know your budget and when INSET times will occur, you can add meat to your own plan.

Carry out an audit

The word audit has been rather overused in education during the last few years. However, if you are starting out in the role of geography coordinator, you may find the process useful and some of the evidence can be placed in your portfolio, described in the next section. Your audit can have a number of sections that help you find out what is happening. They will include

- collecting together all the planning documents ranging from whole school sheets to any lesson planning materials available from staff,
- finding out what geography resources exist, where they are and how or if they are used,
- discovering the levels of expertise and interest among the staff,
- studying any children's work which is available or evidence from previous work, such as folders and photographs, and
- working with some children to sample their levels of current geographical thinking.

Hopefully, such a process will help you discover many positive features as well as those which might benefit from improvement. Your skill in doing this in a non-threatening way will be important. You are not a spy, merely finding out the nature of the baseline from which to develop your work. If you can identify another, perhaps more experienced coordinator, it may be worth talking to them to find out what approaches they found to work well in your school.

Create and build up your own subject portfolio

This shows other people that you are serious about your work and will be a way of organising the large amount of material you will inevitably collect. It will provide evidence to support your aims as well as being a resource to draw on in an inspection and it may be useful in terms of your own

The portfolio might contain some or all of the following:
- the geography policy for your school;
- school policy on educational visits, copies of paperwork, relevant health and safety documents;
- your own action plan detailing proposed developments, INSET, resources, curriculum planning, perhaps set out as a timetable with space for comments on progress;
- copies of the school development plan and budget;
- curriculum planning papers, schemes of work, lesson plans;
- official documents from SCAA, OFSTED, the LEA, the Geographical Association et al.;
- examples of children's work, teachers' records and assessment evidence in geography;
- photographs, videos and IT resources showing evidence of geographical activities e.g. particular topics, links with other places, faxes, videos of residential field visits, evidence and photographs of pupils' work, especially those which cannot readily be stored (Label and date them as they go in order to build up a diary of geographical activities in your school.);
- lists of all geographical resources available in the school and where they are stored;
- resources and contacts beyond the school;
- copies of correspondence with various people and agencies along with lists of names, addresses, phone/fax/e-mail numbers;
- minutes and notes of staff meetings connected with geography;
- papers and ideas you collect on INSET courses;
- list of staff resources e.g. textbooks, handbooks, journals taken and
- things you're collecting for later use e.g. the address of the Central Bureau to apply for funding for your teacher's study visit to Italy!

career development. It should prove to be a central store of materials and continuity for geography, if or when you move to your next school.

Establishing your position within the school

This will extend your professional skills considerably and can be tackled from a number of different starting points. You will need to plan the order in which they may be used and why you think they are worth doing in your school.

Develop your own classroom as an example of good practice in primary geography

You will need to find the precise balance between reality and your ideal or you could risk putting off other teachers, simply through overwhelming them. Demonstrate how enquiry activities can be organised. Show how a range of geographical resources can be used by the children. Celebrate their work in displays, both in your room and around the school. Offering a display to the art coordinator should be popular and give you an opportunity to show what your children have been doing. It can also be a means of showing staff what geographical resources are available and how they might be used.

Use school events to promote geographical education

Your class assembly could explain how your children have been studying the locality around the school. See if the PTA would like a stand from the local rural conservation group at the fete as a way of establishing contact for environmental work required at both key stages.

Look for opportunities to work with staff who may feel threatened

Keep an eye on small details. You may see a member of staff attempt an area of geography in which you know they feel unsure. Offer praise and encouragement to show a genuine professional appreciation of their work. This type of activity will test your interpersonal skills but is essential.

Look out for ways in which other coordinators can help

Asking the information technology coordinator for ideas on using a programmable robot with Key Stage 1 children may help to build a working relationship and indeed help them in the goals for their own subject area. It can also help in the justification and budgeting of resources.

These are just some examples of techniques for managing change and developing interpersonal skills. Listening, empathising, supporting and persuading can all be used where you judge them to be appropriate means of working. Very few people find all of these things easy to do, but have the confidence to try them. If you really believe in the role geography can play in children's development, the effort will be well worth while.

It is also important to accept that you will not have all the answers and ideas. Indeed some of your own assumptions and solutions may be flawed. Ashcroft and Palacio (1997) offer a model of the reflective teacher as one way of developing your interpersonal skills. They suggest that

> *you need to build the sort of relationships with others that will enable them to challenge your assumptions and solutions, such challenges being supportive, rather than destructive, of the relationship. This requires trust on both sides, but can lead to the best kind of professional relationships.*

Talk to the headteacher about the possibility of visiting other classrooms to work alongside staff in geography lessons and ascertain how this can be timetabled in practice. If this is not current school practice, it could be very threatening. Only you will be able to decide if such a technique is possible within the ethos of your school. It is also an excellent way of beginning to assess pupils' learning, progression and continuity and how geographical resources and teaching techniques are used throughout the school.

Looking beyond the school

This is an especially useful skill to develop in terms of geography coordination. We will look in detail at resourcing geography in Part 5 of this book.

- However, at this stage try to find out what help is available from the LEA.

- Are there local organisations who can help you, for example, an urban studies centre?
- Get to know the locality really well.
- Are there contacts within the parents, governors and the wider community who can help develop geographical work?
- Are there links with other local schools or clusters?
- Are there any sources of additional funding to support geography or curriculum development in general available in the region?
- Make contact with the local Geographical Association branch and local interest groups who may offer support. The social aspects of your work are as important as the professional!

All these contacts developed through your social skills should prove helpful in your work at some stage. If you are new to an area or LEA, it is also a good way of getting to meet people and beginning to feel you belong there.

Finally, when you have used these approaches to collect information in the early stages of your role as geography coordinator, you may find it useful to create an action plan. It should be based on both what you have discovered and the longer term ideas you have for how you intend to develop geographical education in the school. You should now be able to prioritise the items in your list both in terms of which ones are needed as a foundation for your work and what you think is practically achievable in your school context. For example, you may have set out with limited ideas on a budget for resources, but discover that at this time of year the school association ask staff if there are any large items of equipment they need for their subject area. Adapt your budget plan accordingly and work hard to obtain your share for geography.

Every action plan will be unique to its school. This is an example of what a geography coordinator's action plan might contain soon after taking up the post.

A geography coordinator's action plan

I need to get to know the local area really well to find out how it may be used.

I'm not sure if I have all the latest guidance papers from OFSTED and SCAA on primary geography. I must get them.

Time to start a portfolio of my work now.

I must talk to the head about setting up a staff development day in geography, perhaps based on some enquiry work in our locality.

There are two members of staff who could help me with raising the profile of geography. How can I work with them?

Information technology is not used at all in geography but the IT coordinator seems very approachable. What project could we build together?

I need to start building a geography resource base. I must talk to the head about where it might be located.

As I'm new to the county, I must contact the local geography adviser to find out what support and INSET may be available.

The geography topic for my class next term — I need to plan and ensure the work will show excellent practice and perhaps create links with some other staff's interests.

Some classrooms have really out-dated geography textbooks in them. How and when can I remove them?

In their book *The Really Practical Guide to Primary Geography*, Foley and Janikoun (1996) suggest ways of setting out a geography coordinator's action plan using headings such as 'Action, How, By whom, By when, Further action' and you could also add 'comments' to these headings.

It is unlikely you will be able to do all these things on your own. Indeed, 'solitary reflection can lead you into a self-serving analysis of problems and to solutions that fit your prejudices rather than the perspectives of others,' (Ashcroft and Palacio, 1997). You may have been able to identify staff and other adults who can help in various ways.

- The English coordinator may be looking for a colleague to develop staff discussion on using speaking and writing skills across the curriculum.

- A senior and influential colleague has local knowledge and ideas on improving funding for geography.

- Your school caretaker is an excellent photographer and may be able to help with making locality resources.

- The Year 5 teacher has now mentioned her Italian link to you three times in a week and has now received a letter from the Italian headteacher!

- A school governor has brought in a leaflet describing a school grounds environmental competition set up by the firm she works for.

These things do happen in school. Part of your skill will be in listening out for possibilties and building relationships, the next stage being to decide which sources of support are most appropriate at a particular time. If you can explain to someone that they have a great idea but also say why you would like to take it up next term and not now, they may see that you are thinking carefully about your job and will listen but not be deflected. Don't get pulled in every direction, but don't be a slave to your action plan. When these possibilities arise stand back and be realistic. You have a class to teach, a life beyond school and whatever you do take on to develop primary geography must be seen to be successful, relevant and enjoyable to everyone involved.

Geography is about people and the world in which they live. Your pupils are some of those people. Discovering their thoughts and ideas about the world will be a very important part of your role as geography coordinator. Wiegand (1993) summarises this very clearly

> *Children already have experience of the world — both direct and indirect — and they use this experience to interpret new experiences. Teachers have a responsibility therefore to establish what the nature of that prior knowledge and experience is, so that it can be built on.*

Chapter 3

Establishing a secure place for geography in the school curriculum

> *The role of the subject coordinator becomes even more crucial, both informally and formally.*   (Chambers and Donert, 1996)

This chapter will look at some practical ways in which you could begin to initiate change based on the confidence and information gained from the earlier stages of your work. It will explain how parts of your action plan can now be developed and new issues will be introduced. Finally, the ideas developed in these first three chapters will be brought together in a sample job description for a geography coordinator, providing a framework through which to view the role you have developed.

So far you will probably have worked with individual members of staff and small groups. At some stage you will want to lead meetings for the whole staff to promote the development of geographical education. If these meetings are successful they will raise the profile of geography, improve staff understanding and confidence and finally, provide a foundation for consensus and ownership of any changes which are to take place. It will rest on your ability to plan and manage meetings.

Managing meetings

Meetings can take up a great deal of time but to little effect. You and your colleagues are busy people, therefore the first set of questions to ask is

- Why do we need to hold a meeting?
- What do I want to happen at the meeting?
- What are my intended outcomes of the meeting?

Many meetings take place when another management strategy could be used. If you are giving information, could this be done more effectively by handing out copies of the information well before the meeting and then using the time together to discuss the content and implications. (Some information won't even need a meeting.)

A clear agenda for your meeting is essential and will act to eliminate confusion or aimless discussions. For example, use a staff meeting to examine the geography schemes of work and identify where information technology and other relevant cross-curricular links exist or might be created. At the end everyone should have a clear idea of what they have learned and what is agreed. Keep the aims of any meeting short and simple. It is far better to move forward in small successful stages rather than to cover too much ineffectively.

Before you plan your staff meetings and INSET events it can be a good idea to try to find out informally how the previous geography coordinator planned these. What did people think about them? Are there any records of what happened? Staff will not want to cover the same ground again unless you can explain why. There is nothing worse than beginning the meeting and have someone say 'well . . . we did this last year' and you not to know about it. If you know, you can have your reasons for revisiting at the ready.

It can also be helpful to set out a possible timetable of events in your action plan. After discussion with the head, you can then offer this at your first meeting with everyone. Ask for their views and any other content they think might be useful. This all helps to create ownership of any discussion and changes. Take notes and ideally send out minutes in whatever way will be non-threatening within your school culture.

There are many types of meetings you could design to promote geography. Study this list and consider which might work in your school, when would they be appropriate and what particular approach would best suit your aims and content:

- whole staff meetings;
- year group meetings;
- key stage meetings;
- staff development days;
- demonstrations, e.g. asking another member of staff to show how they've used an inflatable globe and simple atlases at KS 1;
- workshops; e.g. how can we use the sand tray river model?
- lunchtime drop-ins; e.g. here's our new programmable robot — let's play;
- visitors — advisory teacher, representative from the local development education centre;
- visits to other places: try some staff orienteering in the local park, how can we use the local river?
- videos.

Geography is an active subject often using enquiry approaches and fieldwork. If you can get some of this feel for the subject across in the methods you use in your meetings, it may in turn create change in teacher's own methods. More useful ideas and information on organising and running meetings can be found in *The Primary School Management Book*, (Playfoot, Skelton and Southworth, 1989).

Some of your meetings will focus more on discussion and development of policy while others will be aimed at the practical development of staff skills and confidence. The following three examples may give you some ideas for developing relevant and successful geography-focused meetings and events in your school.

Getting to know the locality

Very few teachers now live in the school's locality. The geography Orders at Key Stages 1 and 2 include a considerable amount of work based on the locality. How much do your staff know about it? Do they use it? Is it planned into schemes of work in a progressive way? A very useful staff development day can be spent as follows:

9.30 am	coffee, welcome, aims of the day, locating small groups to areas, giving out plans, photos, cameras, compasses, notepads etc.
10.00 am	small group fieldwork in the locality, perhaps with groups swapping areas about 11.15 am, or moving to a new area within the locality
12.30 pm	lunch in local pub (Key Stage 2 Gg 9b Settlement 'how land in settlements is used in different ways'!)
1.30 pm	return to school, groups prepare their findings and ideas
2.15 pm	group feedback, showing findings and discussions
3.30 pm	where do we go from here with what our enquiries have found?
3.45 pm	end of day

Doing a SWOT analysis

This is a way of looking at your school's strengths, weaknesses, opportunities and threats in geography. Examples are given in italics. Make a list for your school and compare it with the ideas staff offer when you use this activity.

Strengths are the things your school is good at in geography:
using the locality; carefully designed topics at Key Stage 1; staff willing to be open and honest.

Weaknesses let your school down and prevent good practice in geography:
limited use of information technology; few resources for studying distant localities.

Opportunities are things which exist but are not being used:
a development education centre exists in your city; the local geography adviser would support initiatives in practical ways.

Threats are problems preventing you achieving your objectives.
very tight school budget restriction; majority of staff do not perceive geography to be important.

Ideally a SWOT analysis should involve all the staff. Instead of just explaining the activity and asking staff to do it during a staff meeting, consider other ways of approaching it.

■ Perhaps at an earlier meeting on another subject you (and the head if they are showing active support for your initiatives?) could ask for five minutes to explain what you would like them to do.

■ A week later you have your meeting and staff bring along their ideas. They compare ideas in small groups and write them on four separate pieces of paper headed S, W, O, and T.

■ Compare the ideas as a whole staff and ask them to identify two or three key areas in each section which they think could act as starting points for action.

■ Talk through these points alongside your ideas to help clarify the current situation. This will be a careful balance of helping them achieve ownership and understanding of change while at the same time not compromising the goals and standards you believe to be best practice in primary geography.

Developing staff ideas about geographical enquiry and places

Enquiry is central to good practice in geography. Places are one of the building blocks within the Orders. This activity is designed to get colleagues thinking about what is involved in them using their own experiences as starting points. It is simple and non-threatening. They will be using quite a wide range of geographical skills and you could probably bring these out at the end. The activity could form part of a useful workshop near the start of the school year. It's not meant to be a signal for staff to base planning on their holiday experiences and all the pitfalls of bias and stereotyping which that may create. Rather, it can encourage them to think about how their children, like them, bring a wide range of geographical experiences to school. It can also show how simple resources can start a process of geographical enquiry in which skills, places and themes are integrated and balanced as appropriate. The idea is developed from *Geography in the Early Years*, (Palmer, 1994).

Ask staff well in advance to bring with them a postcard, photograph, map or artefact relating to her or his holiday travels. Hopefully you will get a range of locations from some very near school to the very distant. All will probably reveal how interesting place can be. Place a large sheet of paper next to each item and ask everyone to go around and jot down a question they would like to ask about them. The staff then spend a few minutes talking about their items, answering the questions. Your role is to listen carefully and guide the meeting and to begin to lead colleagues into an understanding of what geographical enquiry is. You may also be able to tease out some of the skills, places and themes being introduced by their questions. They might also begin to see how simple resources can be used to develop clear and focused geographical study. They may also see how they are using their own geographical experiences to help place the new images within a context and framework. The fascination of places and travel should ideally come across. We are quite lucky in that many of our colleagues do travel but this may also mean that for some it is commonplace. This is not so for all of our children. Yet most primary children do have an interest in exploration and places.

This activity is designed to demonstrate how easy it is for good primary geography to begin from simple resources and finding out through enquiry. You might also be able to begin to introduce issues of fieldwork by asking what else we could discover from well organised visits and what other resources will deepen our understanding of these places visited during the holiday.

Strengthening your role

As your role develops within the school there will be a number of activities which you will regularly need to review, develop and adapt. You will adopt them as appropriate to your school, your action plan and the ongoing cycles of change which will take place. This section outlines some of these and discusses their relevance to you as a geography coordinator.

Professional development

In addition to the programme of staff development you will need to review your own professional development.
- What skills do you need to extend?
- How will you keep up to date with developments within the subject?
- Are these part of a wider range of skills within your broader career plan?

If your school has a staff review programme use this to ensure that your interests and those of the school are included. Your levels of job satisfaction are an important factor in the effectivenes of your work.

Curriculum development

Even when you have agreed a geography policy and designed schemes of work, you will need to monitor its actual use and effectiveness. Are the chosen topics really providing opportunities to teach geography? Can the content be covered in the time allocated on paper? You will need to liaise with other subject coordinators and in some schools you may be able to work alongside a whole school curriculum coordinator. This will be a major part of the ongoing development of your role in the school.

Building in flexibility

We have already discussed the fact that the geography Orders allow for flexibility of content within the geography curriculum. This has an important impact on your role. For example, if you can get to know the locality well and watch for proposals and changes, these may provide an excellent way of building real life events into the geography curriculum. Talk to parents, read the local papers and ask the children what's happening in their locality. If you know a year in advance that a piece of derelict land is earmarked for retail development, you can begin to discuss with colleagues how this might be used in one of your locality units of work. They won't be interested if you suggest it two weeks before their project is due to begin. It will also give you a chance to build up resources, make local contacts and prepare possible fieldwork.

We cannot predict unplanned events such as famines or volcanic explosions. You can, however, ensure that, where appropriate, they are included in your children's experiences by doing a number of things. Start to build an ethos where teachers understand the more flexible nature of the geography content requirements. Be alert to unexpected news items that might be relevant to geography and try to collect simple resources which could be used. They may then start to find good sources of materials. One test of your effectivness is when colleagues begin to do this themselves and clearly understand the reasons for including these in their teaching: for instance, they decide to follow an around the world balloon flight with their class each day because they plan to teach specific atlas skills and increase children's locational knowledge of other countries.

School Development Plan

Read the paperwork produced in your school and listen to discussions carefully. Even if some of the management activities seem removed from your role, they can have a strong effect on it as well as providing you with opportunities to develop your subject. For instance, plans to extend the library may give you a chance to suggest ways in which children might be involved in the design. Also, keep an eye on the extent to which your own action plan has realistic links with changes proposed for the school development plan.

More formal monitoring

Your action plan will need to be informed by regular monitoring of everything related to geography. You cannot do everything all the time so decide how it will be best to stage your monitoring and again write this down and include it in your portfolio. This will involve deciding the year groups where you want to study children's work in depth. It might include looking at the development of geographical vocabulary at Key Stage 1, or which geographical skills do children really use during each of their field visits? You will also need to discuss with the headteacher what you are doing and how this information can be built into the wider monitoring work of the school. How will information be stored and reported? S/he might be interested in you making a short presentation to governors a year after your appointment to discuss how geography is developing in the school.

OFSTED

All curriculum coordinators will be involved with OFSTED inspections. If you are appointed after an inspection, it will be important to read the report and be fully involved in any aspects of the action plan requiring your input. If an inspection is to take place in the near future you will need to begin to prepare paperwork and collect evidence to assist the inspection process. Your portfolio will be invaluable before and during an inspection if you have had time to develop it. It can provide evidence of what has occurred in geography and the overall structure of your plans for future developments. Try to read reports from other local schools. Ask your headteacher for copies of useful documents including *Guidance on the Inspection of Nursery and Primary Schools* (1995) and think carefully how the various sections may link with geography. For instance, 'the contribution which the school's links with the community make to pupils' attainment and personal development', (OFSTED, 1995b) could be strong when you involve local people in your locality studies and fieldwork. This aspect of your work is covered in depth in Part 4 of this book.

Cycles of school life

Get to know the patterns of events in the school. What opportunities do these offer for you to raise the quality and profile of geography? This awareness can also help to establish you within a school if you have recently moved to it. Perhaps your class could use an assembly time to show other Key Stage 1 children and staff just what a programmable robot can do in geography; a good way of introducing it soon after it arrives.

Developing resources

This is covered in details in Part 5 of this book and is another central and ongoing part of your work. It is never finished!
- Check resources regularly to remove outdated materials and make running repairs.
- Examine how resources are being used by colleagues.
- How easy is it for staff and children to find and use resources?
- What new commercial materials are being published?
- What is happening in your locality and contrasting locality?
- Monitor spending on your budget and keep a look out for cost effective ways of extending this, for instance special offers in the town centre on photographic enlargements.

Fieldwork and health and safety

With a class commitment, you cannot be expected to go on every field visit. You do need to be aware of when these are happening and be ready to offer support. Also, when they return find time to talk to those who went.

Facilitating school liaison:
- Perhaps some of your children could make simple models which nursery children could use.
- Would a discussion with the secondary school modern languages department help you in writing a letter to the Italian headteacher, and
- their sixth form students could help your children with their European studies.

- Is the area still suitable for the intended work?
- Have new safety issues arisen?
- Are new resources available and might you need to include these in your budget for next year?

It's also important to be aware of health and safety matters. Let the head know that you would be interested in having copies of LEA documents as they arrive. Your interest and being well-informed might prove invaluable and even life-saving at some stage.

School liaison

Find out how links are made with feeder nurseries or schools and the schools to which your children will transfer. Are there ways of developing geographical work through them?

Raising the profile of geography

If you are able to work on some of these aspects of your role at intervals during the year, you will probably be doing an effective job in raising the profile and quality of geography in your school. It will be impossible to do them all at once and in depth. Target the ones which need action because of events beyond your control, OFSTED, for example. Then, use your knowledge of the school and, keeping your own aims for geographical education at the front of your mind, work towards achieving them. Whatever the outside pressures on your role, your own values must stay central and help you keep on course. Whatever you decide to do

 it is assumed that every educational choice *is based upon a* value commitment *to some* interpretative framework *by those involved in the* curriculum process.　　(Van Manen, 1977)

That framework requires a reflective understanding of the nature of the subject and the confidence in using it to make decisions and express them effectively to others. It is the subject of the second part of this book.

Part two

What geography coordinators need to know

Chapter 4
Subject knowledge

Chapter 5
What the coordinator needs to know about current research

Chapter 6
What coordinators need to know about cross-curricular links

Chapter 7
What the coordinator needs to know about fieldwork and the law

Subject knowledge

> ❝ One of the most significant shifts to have occurred in the curriculum in the 1990s is the shift towards the instrumental aims of education.
> (Graves, 1997)

The geography coordinator has a very important role to play in leading the process of how a school comes to define its aims and practice in geographical education. There are still heavy demands on both teacher and curriculum time to cover everything expected in the National Curriculum. The relative status of geography in the primary school is low and has already been discussed. If you are to feel confident in leading this debate it will be helpful to have a clear understanding of

- current thinking about effective practice in geography;
- the interpretation of 'official' requirements;
- a broader context in which to assess this information, along with your own beliefs and values about both geography and education generally.

The aim of this chapter is to explain and discuss the key issues in geography as they stand in the late 1990s. It does not presume previous expertise in geography, but attempts to examine the main 'building blocks' which together form the structure of geography at the present time. However, it also raises questions which only you will be able to answer in the context of your school. While accepting the pressures on schools in terms of expectations, performance etc, this chapter aims to give you the confidence to think beyond the domination of the 'instrumental aims of education' (Graves, 1997) which exist in so much thinking and decision making at the present time. With its less prescriptive content, geography may be one subject you can offer colleagues as a means of re-gaining some of their professional autonomy and opportunity to control the aims and shape of the educational experiences they provide for their pupils.

The aims of geography

> *There are significant omissions from the English and Welsh Statutory Orders for Geography in the National Curriculum. There is no general overview of the nature of geography and its contribution to a child's education. No broad aims are expressed.*
> (Naish, 1997)

It is likely that you will be expected to include the aims of geographical education when you prepare the school geography policy. Perhaps even more important will be your ability to discuss and formulate these ideas in your own mind and with other people. You may be worried about your capacity to do this but you are not alone! There is no one agreed definition of the aims of geography in existence. Different writers and schools of thought will offer their own versions, which all need interpreting in the light of the background from which they come and when they were actually written. The three chapters by Marsden, Walford and Graves (1997) in *Teaching and Learning Geography* give an interesting and concise historical overview of the place of geography in the school curriculum between 1886 and 1997 that may help you to place your own views about the aims of geography in a wider context. If you want to consider learning from a humanities perspective, the first chapter of *Humanities in Primary Education* (Kimber et al. 1995) provides a helpful discussion of the key issues. We are now adding to that story through the way in which we interpret the Orders, along with our professional beliefs. What, therefore, may influence the content and justification of your aims?

You will be constrained by a number of factors. The first is that the school may already have an agreed format in which each subject's aims are described. You will have to adhere to this framework if it is given. Secondly, in a well planned whole school curriculum, no one subject can create its aims without reference to the other subjects and other school policies. You will need to talk to the other curriculum coordinators and senior staff as you develop your aims for geography. The content and philosopy behind your aims will be established from how you interpret the frameworks already present in the school, the degree of flexibility you have in doing this and your ability to act as an agent of change within the school. The following questions are offered as a starting point from which to think about developing your aims within the context of your school.

- Is the curriculum subject led or are there opportunities for appropriate intergration of content from various National Curriculum subjects?
  In practice, this will affect statements you can include about the way in which geography may contribute to children's broader understanding of the world, for example in understanding why places change through history.

- What range of teaching and learning strategies are used?
  If the dominant form is didactic and teacher led, it could result in a geography curriculum in which the transmission of geographical facts might dominate. Is this one of your aims? If not, how can you change it?

- Are children encouraged to ask questions and develop lines of enquiry or is knowledge seen as non-problematic?
  If pupils do not develop these skills in other parts of the curriculum, how can they be developed in geography and will colleagues understand the reasons for this?

- Are pupils and teachers able to make use of a wide range of resources in their study of geography? Will one of your aims be to ensure that this occurs?
  It will require, for example, a range of maps and plans at different scales. Children will be encouraged to use these

in real contexts to learn geographical skills. To what extent will your aims include the use of fieldwork?

■ How will you achieve a balance between human and physical geography? There will be some links here with science.
Human and physical geography are closely linked. Can you work with colleagues to design a range of subject focused and integrated units of work which will allow children to begin to understand these links in the real world?

■ How much factual knowledge of geography is important? To what extent are skills and concepts crucial? To what extent does the development of children's feelings about the world play an important part?
Some locational knowledge is very helpful, for example, what shape are the British Isles? Where is their home located within them? But so are skills: can a child use an atlas to find a map of the British Isles? We all have feelings about places: Where do they feel secure, excited or afraid? Why?

■ The Orders do require children to study environmental issues and consider the effects human activity has on the planet. To what extent will your aims include the study of processes which can become controversial?
Will colleagues and the wider school community agree to including debate about the environment and controversy within the curriculum? Will you be content if it is not included? There are very few other openings in the Orders for such learning experiences to be developed within the primary curriculum.

■ To what extent will you aim for children to learn to begin to understand and respect the ways of life and values of people in other parts of the world, both near and far?
This might include the beginnings of an understanding of how our activities are closely linked and how we all have an effect on other people. It relates well to the broader school curriculum where values and attitudes play an important part.

■ Do you want children to enjoy learning about the world around them?

This will be affected by the extent to which you can draw and build upon their own experiences. The teaching and learning styles of geography lessons will have an effect. For example, a constant supply of photocopied sheets will begin to give them a narrow view of what geographical enquiry really is and certainly limit the development of a wide range of geographical skills.

These questions have been designed to support your thinking on the aims which are important to you and the school. We will return to them in more depth in Part 3 when we consider the design of a whole school policy.

Geographical enquiry

An enquiry approach ... may be defined as one in which the teacher assists pupils to develop the abilities to ask questions and to seek to answer them through investigative work.

(DES, 1990)

The aim is for children to develop a range of skills allowing them to ask questions about the world and have the ability to find and assess the answers. As adults, the more we are able to analyse our environment and make informed decisions, the greater our chance of survival and success in whatever activity we're doing. For instance, when we're looking for a new place to live we could ask the five key questions at the heart of geographical enquiry set by Storm (1989).

1 What is this place like?
2 Why is it like it is?
3 How is it connected to other places?
4 How is it changing and why?
5 What does it feel like to be there?

Since 1989 other authors have developed and extended this basic list of questions (Rawlings, 1992; Catling, 1995; Foley and Janikoun, 1996). The Dearing version of the geography National Curriculum has three clear references to enquiry in the skills section:

1 Observe and ask questions about geographical features and issues.
2 Collect and record evidence to answer the questions.
3 Analyse the evidence, draw conclusions and communicate findings.

The 'ability to undertake geographical enquiry and to use skills' (SCAA, 1997b) is again emphasised in the booklet *Expectations in Geography*, confirming the requirement to plan such work into the primary curriculum.

It may also be helpful to look at the Science and History Orders (DfE, 1995) to see their requirements for enquiry when working on the whole curriculum with colleagues. They may need guidance from you about what geographical enquiry really is and how it can be planned for and carried out with their pupils. To achieve a balanced and realistic view of enquiry it may be helpful to consider some of its main characteristics and decide how these can be best used in your school.

Enquiry methods are an active approach to learning. Although children will learn information during the process, the emphasis will be on developing skills and solving problems.

An enquiry may be small, medium or large and there is a need to aim for a balance as learning experiences are planned. This is important because they can take time, which is in short supply in the primary school. A small enquiry could be based on asking one question about a photograph, taking just one lesson. This is just as valid as a whole term's work on a range of questions about the local environment. Also, with younger children one small question directly related to their own experience will be more relevant and interesting to them.

Ownership of the enquiry questions is important. The skill of teachers is essential here to guide children towards asking geographical questions. If you have a successful and continuous curriculum, Year 6 children may well be able to use the experiences from their earlier guided work in being able to set up and carry out a geographical enquiry of their own. You may need to work alongside colleagues on finding the best balance between teacher-led questioning (open and closed questions) and children posing their own questions.

Why do children need to learn to ask geographical questions? Martin (1995) offers the following reasons:
1   Questioning helps children become independent learners.
2   Developing their own lines of enquiry gives children a sense of involvement in the work and is therefore motivating.
3   Children's own questions can often stimulate a line of enquiry the teacher might not have thought of.
4   Children's questions are a good indicator of their present level of knowledge and understanding.
5   Asking questions is part of the enquiry process and therefore a requirement of the National Curriculum.

Martin (1995) suggests young children learn through action and talk and within the discussions two tiers of questioning may be helpful. Level one questions deal with naming, description and memory: *What is the river called? Where are the factories along it?* Level two questions focus on looking at patterns, suggesting explanations and making predictions: *Where is the river most polluted? Why is it polluted? What might happen in the future?*

The enquiry process can follow a number of stages. The content and depth of each one will vary with the children following the activity. The enquiry route below is adapted from National Curriculum Council INSET Resources (NCC, 1993).

Existing knowledge ➔
Asking questions which will help children understand geographical concepts ➔
Planning a set of investigations to ensure relevant data is collected and skills developed. ➔
The investigation will follow the plan, record findings and decide what geographical evidence has emerged. ➔
Evaluation will assess how good the results are and what new questions may need to be asked. ➔
This process should lead to children gaining new levels of understanding and knowledge. ➔

It's perhaps reassuring that SCAA (1997b) include *knowledge and understanding of environmental relationships and issues* within a booklet on expectations in geography at Key Stages

Enquiry is based on asking geographical questions. This example is given to start you thinking about possibilities in your locality.
A piece of derelict land near your school is put up for sale. Pupils begin by asking the question *What used to be there?* Research into old photographs, maps, newspapers and talking to local residents gives some answers. The next stage is to find out why the land use changed and to investigate what the land is like now. This might include its function as a wildlife habitat.

- What will it be used for in the future?
- What would the pupils like to see there?
- What is needed in the locality?
- What is actually going to happen to the land?

These questions are based on pupils' first-hand experience of the locality and geographical resources are developed from local sources.

1 and 2 and the Curriculum Council for Wales (1991) offered guidance on possible questions to develop effective enquiry work around issues:

1   What is the issue?
2   What are its geographical aspects?
3   Where are the issues taking place?
4   What is the place like?
5   What are the background factors to the issue?
6   What groups and individuals are involved?
7   What views do they hold?
8   What attitudes and values underlie these views?
9   What alternative solutions are there?
10   What are their advantages and disadvantages?
11   What are your feelings about the issue?
12   How will a decision be made?
13   Who will make it?

(CCW, 1991)

As you get to know your locality and become more confident in building this type of study into your work, your pupils should begin to learn that events happen and places change for a variety of reasons. Perhaps most important, they will learn that they can have an influence on how things might be in the future.

What might a geographical enquiry in your locality look like?

Asking the questions
Children from a new housing estate are now coming to our school. They have to cross a busy road. The council have agreed to employ a new crossing patrol person.
Where will be the best place for that person to supervise children crossing the road?
Where are the children coming from?
How easily can drivers see them in different places?
Will the steep hill affect how easily drivers can stop?
Do drivers really keep to the 30mph speed limit in the area?

Planning
What will be the best ways of getting answers to our questions?
How will children collect and record the information?
What geographical skills and concepts can be developed through these activities?

The investigation
Which parts of the road really do give drivers the best view of the crossing?
Finding out where the children are coming from by plotting their addresses on local street plans.
Asking them to draw their journeys to school.
Devising and carrying out tests to measure the speed of vehicles.

> *Evaluation*
>
> Looking at all the evidence to decide the best location for the crossing.
>
> Ranking the possible sites by giving weightings to the various reasons.
>
> Considering the possibilities from the point of view of children, parents, drivers etc.
>
> Inviting the local planning/road safety officer to discuss their findings and to ask where they are planning to locate the patrol.
>
> Deciding on a final location.
>
> Perhaps one year later it might be possible to re-visit the issues when the children are older and evaluate the crossing by asking more demanding questions to promote progression in their enquiry work.

The use of key questions through enquiry methods can be used in a wide range of geographical work. They can be located within the units of work you develop to cover the requirements to teach the skills, places and themes sections of the geography Orders in a meaningful and interesting way.

Skills, places and themes

The geography orders for both Key Stages 1 and 2 are set out under three headings: skills, places and themes. Teachers have now had some time to work with these in planning the curriculum. Unfortunately, these three headings are not especially helpful in this process and can cause confusion, particularly with teachers who feel less confident in teaching geography. In your role as coordinator, you may well have two main jobs to do here. The first will be staff development to improve teachers' understanding of subject knowledge and precisely what is meant to be done within these sections. The second job may be to work alongside colleagues at all levels of planning to ensure that geographical experiences are structured around appropriate mixes of skills, places and themes within, where possible, an enquiry approach.

Skills, places and the four thematic studies at Key Stage 2 are not intended to be taught as study units, similar to those prescribed in the history Orders. When you are planning topics or units of work, you need to consider which aspects from the three parts can be blended together to form a set of experiences which have a distinct geographical focus. 'It is vital to integrate place, skills and themes', (Ranger, 1995). Some teachers find it helpful to imagine three spotlights shining onto a stage. They are labelled skills, places and themes.

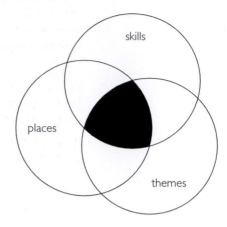

The shaded part where all three overlap may be imagined as the topic itself. It can contain just the relevant parts of the skills, places and themes sections. Other topics will contain different aspects of them and perhaps continue to include some of those already in other topics.

One effective way to begin using skills, places and themes for planning is to decide on a place focus for a study. Move on to consider what lines of enquiry can effectively be developed through teacher guided work. Then decide which geographical skills children will be learning and extending. It is quite possible to integrate one or more of the geographical themes into this place study as well. In this way you will be making all aspects of geographical work relevant and supportive of each other. It can perhaps be made clear if we think about how an example of poor geography planning might look: a lesson is planned in which children will be given a workcard to learn some isolated skills in using an atlas. No reference is made to places or themes, simply the rote learning of some geographic skills. However, if these atlas skills were planned into a topic on Water, the same children might be required to use an atlas to find their local river, the rivers in the distant locality they study and perhaps even developing a line of enquiry such as 'how do people use the river in each locality?'

Your role as coordinator will be to make sure that the range of geographical experiences provides opportunities for a balance of skills, places and themes to be built into each of them. You will also need to check that they provide for continuity and progression. For instance, will the use of maps in the various topics ensure that children are practising and developing their map reading and making skills?

It is quite acceptable for some topics or units of work to have a particular focus based on one of the themes. You may decide that the local river provides a rich source of geographical experiences and therefore one unit for Key Stage 2 will be based on fieldwork and enquiry and entitled 'Rivers' just as the thematic study is called. However, this will also give you many opportunities to plan in the use of geographical skills. As it is your local river, you will be able to develop the place requirements very easily. The best planning could also include some reference to rivers in a contrasting locality studied in depth elsewhere in the timetable. In this way your pupils will hopefully be having experiences which allow them to begin to recognise patterns and processes as they build their knowledge and understanding of various places. Good practice will also give children a chance to study the themes at a variety of scales from local to global. In Part 3 of this book we consider examples of how this integration of skills, places, themes and enquiry can take place in practice.

Selecting geographical topics

The above section began to highlight the importance of choosing geographical topics with great care. This will be another important role for you to play and is one of the foundations needed for really effective geographical education. In an ideal world you would be able sit down with colleagues and design the curriculum afresh with you looking closely at the interests of geography. Sadly, this is very unlikely! In reality you will probably identify the following constraints:
- a two or three year planning cycle already in operation;
- topics or units of work already defined, some of which may be very unsuitable for geography and really part of the pre-National Curriculum history of the school;

■ school commitment to topics in terms of resources purchased, and

■ an existing power base and pecking order of subjects.

If you are not happy with the situation you inherit, one of the most effective starting points is to be brave and begin to discuss the actual topics with colleagues. SCAA (1995b) uses the phrase 'units of work' and suggests these can be continuing and blocked and *that both types of unit will draw, in the first instance, on work from a single subject or aspect of the curriculum.* Some could be linked with other subjects. You will need to examine whether or not these existing units of work can actually provide opportunities for geographical learning experiences. For instance, some schools have misread the requirements on studying distant places at Key Stage 2 and have built in a half term's work on all of 'The Caribbean' rather than choosing an actual locality to study within it. Looking at the geographical units of work, do they really allow chances for progress and continuity in children's learning? Are fieldwork opportunities built into this overall set of units? It is also still possible to find topics which date back thirty years and have simply been built into the new requirements with little thought as to why and how they can offer suitable learning experiences. Within these units of work there should be opportunities to study the range of localities as prescribed in the Orders.

Localities

 A locality is a small area comparable with the catchment area of the school. When the contrasting locality is selected, focus on an area of this size allows depth of study and direct comparison with the children's own local area. (SCAA, 1997a)

Many school plans still expect too large an area to be studied. Check this in your school. Your local area should be similar in size to both the other UK locality and that in another country. Do bear in mind that the size of the locality studied at Key Stage 1 is smaller than at Key Stage 2.

There are a number of reasons for studying localities, Catling (1995) explains they enable children to:

- develop knowledge and undertanding of what each locality is like, in particular their own locality through fieldwork;
- be able to compare the localities they study with each other;
- develop their geographical skills through the study of localities; and
- examine geographical themes through the context of localities.

This article in *Primary Geographer* gives very useful and detailed ideas on choosing, comparing and studying localities.

If you decide that the locality elements of the curriculum need improving, your first job as coordinator is to get to know your locality really well. Incidentally, you really will need to keep up to date and audit your locality on a regular basis: your findings could be the starting point for very valid enquiries into change. Decide what it will include and then you may have to develop some staff INSET along the lines described in Part 1 of this book. This audit and INSET work should help everyone to see what aspects of skills, themes and enquiry can be done well in the area. Find out about your locality from the children (Bowles, 1995). When you have some ideas on this, a contrasting UK locality needs to be chosen. It does not need to be far away or exotic. Indeed, if it is quite close to your school, it may enable fieldwork to be done relatively easily and cheaply. This locality should allow children to study features which contrast with where they live. If you work in a hilly, inland, urban, industrial setting you may decide to choose a village in a flat, rural coastal area. Sweasey (1997) offers practical ideas for studying contrasting UK localities.

Published resources will probably be very limited. You could choose a locality on which a commercial pack has been produced: you may well have to use one of these for your contrasting locality abroad. So, an interesting contrast to these could be provided for your UK locality if you can make contact with a school in a suitable location. There are a number of advantages in this:

- As each school builds its locality resources, it can make two copies of everything and swap them with their partner school.
- Resources can be kept up-to-date quite easily if both schools cooperate well.
- Pupils in both locations can become involved in answering enquiry questions raised by their partner school.
- It provides a practical mechanism for getting pupils involved in their locality and can enable members of the wider community to contribute to your work.
- If fieldwork is planned in, the partner school can provide useful local knowledge and perhaps even practical help with facilities such as toilets.
- The information can feel more relevant because real people are involved and it's not just coming from a pack, TV programme or textbook.
- Such a link can provide opportunities to build in other aspects of the curriculum in relevant ways. For instance, English and IT Orders can be addressed when pupils word process or e-mail questions and information to each other.
- It brings geography to life.
- It's actually far more interesting and rewarding for everyone involved.

If you are prepared to put the effort into creating and coordinating such a link, its innovative nature can help you raise the profile of geography both in the school and the wider community. If done well, it also confirms to OFSTED the school's commitment to active involvement with the wider world.

Links with a contrasting locality can be made in various ways:
- A personal contact of your own in a suitable area.
- A personal contact of a member of staff: this is useful in getting other people involved.
- Your LEA may have connection with another authority.
- The Geographical Association has a list of schools wanting to make links with other parts of the country.

- Using your home page on the web to ask for a partner school.
- If you're still a student, keep in touch with friends who are going to teach in another part of the country. They may just find a job in a suitable location.

Choosing a locality beyond the UK can be done using the ideas above but it may not be as easy to make links with a school. This is where other help can be useful:

- Does your county/borough council have a twinning arrangement with another country? Their twinning officer, or person responsible for European initiatives may be able to help.
- Your local university or training college is probably part of a network with educationalists and schools in other countries. It may be worth contacting them or talking to tutors when they visit students.
- The Central Bureau for Educational Visits has excellent facilities for schools wanting to develop links and partnerships.

Europe is mentioned here because teachers often miss two points in the Orders. The first is that the locality overseas at Key Stage 1 could certainly be in Europe. The second is that at Key Stage 2 they state that for the study of the themes 'contexts should include the United Kingdom and the European Union' (DfE, 1995). Halocha (1997a) discusses the practicalities and opportunities for developing a European dimension in the primary school.

While locality studies are central to primary geography, children would gain a very unrealistic view of the world if they were studied in isolation. 'All localities need to be set in the context of the wider region and country' (SCAA, 1997a). Part of your work will be in supporting staff to do this. One way is to help them begin to recognise opportunities. For instance, if a class is studying the car factory in your locality, they could investigate where in the UK the various parts come from and which countries the finished cars are exported to.

Space and flexibility within your curriculum

We have seen that the geography Orders specify the progress and expectations of primary children. They are summarised (SCAA, 1997a) as:

■ knowledge and understanding of places;

■ knowledge and understanding of patterns and processes;

■ knowledge and understanding of environmental relationships and issues;

■ ability to undertake geographical enquiry and to use skills.

The choice of content and precise locations for this learning are for each school to decide. As geography coordinator you will be working on this with your colleagues. They will need your support and advice. They are busy people and will probably want you to make some of the decisions. This is part of your job but you will be doing an even better job if they gradually gain the confidence to realise their potential for identifying and using opportunities as they arise. This is not advocating a return to the days when the arrival of a flat hedgehog would determine the rest of the primary school day! It is suggesting that when interesting events take place at home and in the wider world, teachers can spend a short time building them into the school day, knowing the geographical reasons for doing this.

It also includes the possibility that unexpected changes will happen in your locality. If the precise content of the schemes of work can be designed to ensure they state the geographical aims you wish to achieve, while leaving the aspects of the content for staff to decide in their medium term planning, you will ensure that the geography curriculum is relevant and up to date. If you can build staff confidence to do this and offer practical support, you may also find that teachers see geography as a more interesting subject to teach because they do not have to repeat the same content every year. That can be left to some other subjects. Your job will then be to monitor what is taught and how continuity and progression are ensured.

As a coordinator you can lead by example. Ask the headteacher if you can have a display board in a prominent

Chambers and Donert (1996) suggest a sequence through which pupils could develop skills and attitudes to help them begin to understand people's values and points of view and how to analyse issues:
1   Awareness of the issue.
2   Identifying the key interest groups.
3   Understanding the different points of view.
4   Identifying their value positions.
5   Proposing various solutions.
6   Evaluation of the proposals.
7   The personal involvement and action of the pupils.

place for a term. In one school a coordinator asked lorry drivers in a local trans-European haulage firm to send postcards to the school as they drove around Europe. The resulting active display raised much interest and certainly got children and adults asking many geographical questions. If you have to lead assembly times when a part or all of the school are together, can you build in current world events to illustrate the themes you are expected to cover?

Beyond the geography Orders

The very nature of the content and methodology of geography means that it can be linked to other subjects, cross-curricular themes and broadly related fields such as human rights. We have already considered the time and content pressures in primary schools, but if you are to be effective in your role, it may be worth thinking beyond the geography Orders. Any curriculum is a result of the political and social values and pressures of its era. Some things are included in it but many are left out. The final part of this chapter outlines some areas which can have important links with geography. They may be starting points for discussion with colleagues as to how broader issues can be integrated within the legally required framework. Indeed, you may well decide that this minimum provides a basic diet for survival but the addition of related studies helps to create a richer and more human set of experiences.

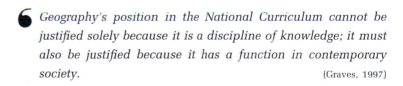 *Geography's position in the National Curriculum cannot be justified solely because it is a discipline of knowledge; it must also be justified because it has a function in contemporary society.*
(Graves, 1997)

Part of that function may be to consider how the world will develop in the future. Hicks (1994) offers a range of reasons for engaging children in thoughts about the future and suggests many practical classroom activities for developing these. They can build very effectively into the thematic work at both key stages. For instance at Key Stage 1 Lewis (1996) considers how a picture book may be used to help children think about how fast the world is changing but keeping it firmly rooted in their own experience.

Geography uses many resources. Children examine photographs, videos, maps and plans. Visitors come to school and people are interviewed on field visits. Increasingly CD-ROMs are searched for information and e-mails are exchanged. All of these activities can be used to develop children's critical awareness of the accuracy and bias of information they can obtain. Media awareness is not a distinct part of the National Curriculum but the English Orders are clear about the need for pupils to *distinguish between fact and opinion* and *consider an argument critically* (DfE, 1995). Geography can provide interesting and relevant sources to be used in such work. The growing range and access to various media also means that children need to be confident in asking questions, selecting appropriate sources and critically assessing them.

If we develop thinking about the future, it may be related to work on citizenship and human rights. This is often linked with the study of issues and enquiries. They are listed in the Order, for instance, we are required to teach pupils about issues arising from the way in which land is used (9c). And if you are to develop enquiry work and examine issues in geography it will be impossible to avoid bringing values into the curriculum.

- Why is it worth asking what gets dumped in the local quarry?
- Does it make any difference if we stop buying hardwood products?
- How can we really help people in places affected by famine?
- Do we really care about what our town will be like in five years' time?
- What are our parents going to do when the local factory closes?
- How can we best use our grant to improve the school grounds?
- What can we do to make it safe for children to walk to school alone?

These are some of the many value-laden questions which geography can help us to answer. Part of your role as geography coordinator is to create a curriculum in which learning is meaningful and helps children develop as human beings. We have perhaps become obsessed with the practicalities of managing the National Curriculum. But it is only a part of the whole curriculum. Graves (1997) puts this clearly in perspective and some of your work can be to guide busy colleagues into considering that:

 the curriculum is a means to an end and not an end in itself. The end is the development of those competencies and qualities of mind that will produce a citizen able to earn his or her living as well as being capable of critical thought.

(Graves, 1997)

Chapter 5

What the coordinator needs to know about current research

> *As teachers of geography we need to be made aware of the cognitive factors and processes operating in or missing from our teaching/learning environment.* (Gonzalez and Gonzalez, 1997)

Children appear to learn about the world in many different ways. They come to school with varied experiences of people and places. In school you organise further geographical learning activities for them. But what can we glean from our understanding of how children's minds develop and the effects of our teaching? Many research findings exist in this field. An awareness of research findings can enable you to:

- discuss geographical education with more confidence;
- provide evidence to assist in making decisions about planning and teaching strategies;
- create a framework for assessment of children's progress.

The aims of this chapter are to:

- provide an introduction to research and key references in geographical education;
- raise some issues which may be related to decisions you have to make;
- stimulate your interest and raise your confidence in this area.

The research field is extensive and a short chapter such as this can only provide an introduction. The references have been carefully chosen to allow you develop your readings in some key areas appropriate for your work.

Major theoretical influences

As in so many aspects of primary education, Piaget has had an influence on our understanding of how children learn and the implications of this for our teaching. Piaget (1929) began his work investigating what aspects of the world children were interested in. Later (Piaget and Weil, 1951) he developed his ideas into children's views about the 'homeland' and its relationship to other countries. Further research (Piaget and Inhelder, 1956) demonstrated how children begin to understand the positions of objects in a spatial sense. In much of the evidence presented he suggests that children's understanding of spatial concepts develop through a series of stages.

However, 'Piaget's work is not without its critics. Although his ideas are powerful, there are substantial objections to his methodology', (Wiegand, 1992). In particular Vygotsky (1979) argues that Piaget's stages are not natural processes but 'historically and socially determined'. He suggests that children's cognitive development will be affected by the range and type of materials they experience. They will also be influenced by social and cultural situations. McGarrigle and Donaldson (1974) re-examined the experimental processes Piaget used and raised further questions about their accuracy. Research on the relevance of Piaget's stages to geographical education has been wide. Darvizeh and Spencer (1984) suggest that we may understand children's growing ability to analyse the spatial world better in terms of how they are taught to apply strategies for reading the environment for appropriate information. Spencer et al. (1989) offer a detailed and informative discussion of more recent research into children's development of spatial knowledge and understanding. Palmer (1994) suggests that the wide range of research evidence 'in this general field of environmental cognition and development of spatial awareness is that young children are remarkably good at learning.'

The key questions for a geography coordinator are therefore:

■ How far do the theories of Piaget, Bruner, Vygotsky and those who challenge their ideas, relate to the practical decisions we have to make in school?

■ How can we identify and build upon what children already know and understand about the world?

■ To what extent is their learning sequential?

■ How do the quality of learning resources and the social environment affect their learning?

■ What implications do the answers to these questions have for the way in which we design the geography curriculum?

Wiegand (1992) and Palmer (1994) provide more detailed discussions about the key theoretical perspectives and how they influence our thinking about children's understanding of places and the development of spatial cognition in the early years. These texts also provide useful references to take your own reading interests further if you wish. Within this broad theoretical framework, a great deal of research is currently taking place and the next section outlines some major areas in which this is happening and how they might link with your work as geography coordinator.

Some recent developments in geographical research

It would be impossible to discuss all current research in a short chapter. The following examples have been chosen to demonstrate a range of recent research interests and their relevance to your work.

Palmer (1992, 1993) is developing an ongoing research study examining the growth of knowledge and concern for the environment in both children and adults. This is a cross-cultural study taking place in both Co. Durham, England and California, USA. The data arising from this research 'provides insights into the development of basic concepts needed to understand our geographical world and related environmental issues. We are also provided with insight into the development of awareness of problems and concerns for the world', (Palmer, 1994). As the results are published teachers will be able use this growing understanding of how pupils' knowledge and attitudes towards the environment may be effectively developed.

Mackintosh (1997) is developing research in pupil's understanding of rivers through examining the effects of teaching methods used in helping children understand physical processes. She argues that some methods allow children to learn river facts by rote but they do not understand how a river works. By using the constructivist approach developed in science and mathematics, it may be possible to devise activities and experiences which will enable children to actually begin to understand how the world works, rather than collecting geographical facts. As a coordinator, you may be able to discuss these ideas with science and maths coordinators in your school to see if, perhaps, progress and continuity of teaching methods might be examined, using the constructivist approach as a starting point. Bell and Gilbert (1996) discuss these ideas in greater depth.

We take for granted that young children have some experience and understanding of their local environment. Research by Matthews (1992) revealed that children's experience of places further away from home increased with age and were affected by three main factors:

- parental attitudes, for instance on the extent children were allowed to roam;
- physical ability, e.g. to ride a cycle;
- the nature of the environment, perhaps the effects of hills, river boundaries.

Evidence also suggested that boys produced more extensive, detailed and accurate maps. Such research may inform ways in which differentiation is built into geographical activities, as well as your role in monitoring equal opportunities within the school.

The current concern regarding children's freedom of movement is being examined by Hillman (1998) and has interesting connections with Matthews' work. Hillman's findings from an extensive study about children's experiences of the environment around their homes in the late 1990s suggests 'we are breeding a generation of "battery-reared children" qualitatively very different from the previous generations of "free-range" children'. It raises questions about the knowledge and understanding of the locality which children bring to school and by implication, the curriculum you plan to develop these.

Wiegand's recent research into children's understanding of the world (1998) has studied how shape, size, position, proportion and information differs on various map projections. This can create confusing and inconsistent images for children. To assist children in learning the skills to understand and interpret these, his findings suggest that more effective teaching will take place if children 'use the globe and world map together throughout the primary years and beyond' (Wiegand, 1998). If you wish to apply these findings in your school, what implications might they have for working with colleagues on developing their teaching strategies and the resources needed? You can become involved in active research by making links with people working in this field. The next section provides some ideas for creating such relationships.

Research groups

Various groups of people are undertaking research in geographical education. Teachers who are interested in finding out more about the effects of their work undertake projects of various sizes. These are often connected with INSET and higher degree course programmes. Some fascinating work is carried out in schools by such teachers, the problem is that very few of their findings reach a wide audience. The difficulty of bringing the results of this research together means that broad trends and emerging patterns are hard to identify. The implications of this for you as a coordinator are that you could try to become familiar with courses your colleagues have already attended and also talk to inservice teaching staff in your LEA and local colleges. They can often put you in touch with useful contacts. For instance, a teacher in a local school may have completed an MEd thesis which critically examines how work in a local field studies centre affected children's understanding of environmental issues. You may be able to draw ideas from this to assist your school's use of the centre.

Lecturers in university departments of education and training colleges are required to conduct research as part of their professional work. Some is small scale research while others are able to attract considerable sums of money for nationally and internationally significant studies. More of their work is published in journals, books and conference papers. This can have a number of implications for you as a coordinator. There may be lecturers in local institutions wanting to develop school-based research work who may be very interested to hear from teachers who want to understand better what is happening in their school. Academic staff often have experience of bidding for research funds and their status and previous work can assist this. If you can make contact with such staff your school may become involved in work which not only feeds into a greater understanding of your school, but can bring money, additional teaching resources and possibly a raising of geography's profile.

Your school may be involved with initial teacher education programmes. Students often have to research and write a dissertation in a particular subject or aspect of education. Talk to students, visiting tutors and your school's partnership coordinator to find out what the students have to do in their course. If you know well in advance it may be possible to negotiate a research question which satisfies their course requirements and produces useful data to inform your decision-making. They will be pleased to have found a research base and you may be able to achieve something which would not have been possible without their input of time.

Local education authorities also have research interests. Get to know the geography/humanities advisers and advisory teachers. Find out who else may be interested within the LEA. For instance, an industry/education liaison officer may well be able to involve you in a funded 'schools into industry' project. If you are willing to become involved in researching the work, funds could be available.

OFSTED and SCAA carry out a great deal of research in schools. Summaries of the results are published regularly, for example *Geography. A review of inspection findings 1993/94* (SCAA, 1995a). They are sent to schools but do not always reach teachers. Let your headteacher know that you really do want to see them. Ask for new ones to be passed on to you and see if you can get previous publications. As a coordinator, you need to be aware of their findings for two reasons. First, it keeps you fully informed about what is happening in schools at a national scale, which allows you hold up a mirror to what you do. Second, you gain a clear impression of the importance OFSTED and SCAA place on these issues. It means you can review your practice in the light of these and it helps in keeping your school policies broadly in line with legal requirements. You can also discuss trends in an informed manner with senior staff, parents and governors. Harrison (1998) suggests that using a 'ghost' such as OFSTED requirements may be a useful and unassertive way of starting a change process in school, but accepts it can also breed resistance. You need to understand your work context.

Non-governmental organisations (NGOs) also carry out educational research. Oxfam, Worldwide Fund for Nature and many others have research projects in action. Most have educational newsletters and journals. If you are interested in keeping up-to-date with developments and perhaps becoming involved, ask to go on their mailing lists. As well as possibly responding to one of their initiatives, you may find from reading their publicity that they would be very interested in hearing about what you are doing in school. Primary teachers are good at under-estimating the quality, excitement and importance of their work. Publicise what you do well and look out for new ways of doing it!

Keeping up to date with research

The Geographical Association is producing a new book provisionally called *Researching Primary Geography*

(Scoffham, 1998). At the time of writing (Autumn, 1997) it is hoped this book will be published about the same time as the book you are currently reading. Scoffham's book will contain articles reporting the very latest work in primary geography research set in the context of society today. It is intended to support teachers through the period of the post-Dearing review and beyond. The summaries of Wiegand's and Hillman's work cited above are drawn from this book.

The Geographical Association has supported the creation of a national *Register of Research in Primary Geography*. Details of it are included in the chapter on resources later in this book. Everyone interested in this area of research is encouraged to have their work recorded on the register. The aim is create a large database of work being done by teachers, student teachers, teachers on INSET courses, advisers and academics. As a busy teacher you could access this information to assist you in your work as a coordinator. You have 'a need to know more about children's geographical perceptions . . . this requires research based on a foundation of sound observation from many classroom sources, supported by rigorous analysis' (Bowles, 1996). The research register exists to help you and your contribution will also be very welcome.

Educational research into the role of subject coordinators in primary schools

Teachers are busy people and in any job it's easy to get swept along with the pace of work and everyday demands. It's not always possible to stand back, reflect on what we're doing, consider what is going on in other schools and, perhaps, at a national level. As the role of subject coordinator has become more important in primary schools, a number of research projects have begun to examine what they do and the broader implications of their work. This section will discuss some recent evidence and may help you review your current position and suggest things you might do in the future. Some of the findings may be re-assuring in that you are far from alone in many aspects of your work.

It may be worth thinking about the extent to which Webb and Vulliamy's research affects your work. Sometimes if you can begin to untangle the pressures, it becomes possible to target areas to work on. You can't achieve everything at once, but prioritising your needs may be an important first step. It may also indicate some of your needs. For instance,

- can the headteacher arrange for you to get some teaching experience in another Key Stage?
- Is the head aware that two members of staff resent your role because you are a relatively new entrant to the profession?

All these are real issues and will affect how well you can do your job.

Webb and Vulliamy's (1996) research into the role of the primary school coordinator was conducted in fifty schools. They identified four main issues stated by coordinators as having a restrictive effect on their work:

- the level of subject expertise in their curriculum area;
- insufficient time to carry out all the things they believed were important;
- power relations in the school;
- in primary schools, coordinators were often aware of their lack of expertise in the Key Stage where they did not teach.

Bell (1997) has developed an on-going research project examining what curriculum coordinators do in primary schools and some of the implications for children's learning and the curriculum. Research has focused on the actual activites undertaken by coordinators and how long they spend on them. Coordinators across a range of subjects were asked to keep daily records and early results indicate that they spend almost five hours per week on their coordinator's role, which is in addition to their normal class commitments. Some interesting patterns emerge when this time allocation is examined in detail.

Coordinators were found to spend 44 per cent on professional development. This included activities such as attending courses, collecting information and advice relevant to their subject and getting support from other colleagues such as the headteacher.

Twenty-two per cent was spent on managing subject resources. This work revolved around preparing orders, repairing, sorting, tidying and generally looking after materials connected with the subject. Bell argues that many of the tasks done in this category could be carried out by a technician/general assistant/parent. It may be worth studying the time you actually spend on these jobs to understand the extent to which they dominate your time. If they do, is there any way of getting some help in order to free you up to do some of the more professional aspects of your work?

Twenty-one per cent of time was spent in planning. Within this, Bell found that teachers spent more than 50 per cent of this time planning at home because they said they could work there with fewer interruptions. If you find yourself in the same situation, it may be worth asking what the effect is of you working alone. Is there a case in your situation to involve colleagues more in the planning process? Bell suggests that if this is the dominant model, too much planning may be done in isolation, perhaps resulting in less consultation and repetition of work in some areas.

Eight per cent of their coordinator's time was spent in supporting colleagues. It is perhaps worth thinking about your own views of this part of the data. Is this what you might expect? Does it match your own experience? Is it enough? If it happens this way, why? Bell also examined the data in more depth by breaking up the time allocations of tasks into those which were done in blocks of less than fifteen minutes duration. Twenty-four per cent of the time supporting colleagues was done in such periods. Examples would include brief chats at lunchtime. Is this how you work? How effective is it? Do you repeat a lot of what you do?

Five per cent of time was spent on evaluation. This included looking at children's work, observing teaching and record keeping. If we are to see coordinators as having a monitoring role for their subject, this figure may appear to be rather low. It is quoted simply to start you thinking about how you divide up the time you spend in your role as coordinator. How appropriate is the balance in your school? Does it match the needs of what your priorities are at the present time?

Richie's (1997) research into the nature and effectiveness of primary school subject coordinators supports many of Bell's (1997) findings. Managing resources and advising colleagues take up most time while assessment and monitoring take the least. He also studied the constraints which coordinators felt were imposed on them. They included:

Insufficient time was almost unanimously reported, with non-contact time as the main concern.

Lack of opportunity to get into other classrooms for a variety of reasons such as teacher support and monitoring. This may be one reason why monitoring and evaluation rarely happens.

Evidence is also offered about the time constraints in primary schools and the effects of major curriculum development programmes such as the National Literacy Project. This is, perhaps, an important issue for the geography coordinator. The domination of mathematics and English in the timetable, the perceived status of various subjects and the pressure created by SATs all help to push subjects such as geography into a minor position. Perhaps one of your functions as a geography coordinator is to reinforce the high profile of geography in your school. Being well informed about current research in education may help you with this work.

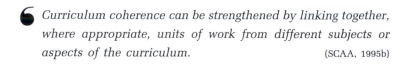

| Chapter 6 | What coordinators need to know about cross-curricular links |

Curriculum coherence can be strengthened by linking together, where appropriate, units of work from different subjects or aspects of the curriculum. (SCAA, 1995b)

Introduction

HMI (1989) findings from the National Primary Survey stated that 'in most schools there was a tendency for geography to lose its distinctive contribution and to become a vehicle for practising skills related to language and art'. It is perhaps worth quoting once again from this often quoted report because it helps to place your current work within a broader context. As a result of this survey the implementation of the National Curriculum meant that primary school pupils had an entitlement to clearly identifiable geography elements in their curriculum. Teachers were encouraged to ensure that clear geographical elements of work could be identified whether they were taught as a separate subject, or linked in some way to other curriculum areas.

Times have moved on. Although there is still considerable scope for improvement, primary children do receive more geographical education than in the 1970s. But the Dearing review of the National Curriculum did make some significant changes. There is still a statutory requirement to teach the geography Orders, however, the greatest emphasis is clearly on English, mathematics, science and information technology. They are high status subjects both in terms of time allocated and assessment needs. There are concerns that the review of the Dearing five year curriculum may reduce the geography requirements still further, with pressure for more specialist teaching in the core subjects. Fewer new teachers are being trained as geography specialists.

All of this has an effect on how you will manage geography within the whole school curriculum. Do you decide that it should be a clearly identifiable subject? Will its position be strengthened if it is carefully linked with other appropriate subjects in your whole school planning or will this return it to its vague and unclear position of the 1970s? You need to have a clear picture of the advice and messages coming from SCAA, OFSTED and other sources. You also need to think about how geography can best make its contribution to all other aspects of life in your school. You cannot work in isolation.

The next section discusses advice from various sources. The final section takes a realistic look at ways in which links may be made based on this advice and the interpretation you make of what is possible in your school.

Interpreting recommendations

One of the pressures on coordinators is their accountability for their decisions and actions. The best primary teachers also have beliefs about their view of good practice. It's not always easy to reconcile this with legislation and guidance from various sources. As you read these sections try to decide where you stand on the issues raised and what you might do in your school.

The common requirements of the geography Orders clearly state that

Use of language
and
Information technology

must be planned into geographical work. This is statutory and SCAA (1997d) agree that speaking, listening, reading and writing may be developed by geography because 'it can provide a wide range of classroom and fieldwork experiences in which to develop these skills'. When you are designing or revising your whole school policy for geography check that they are included. Be clear about how progress and continuity can be identified. For instance, how will geographical writing become more demanding through the key stages? Can a path be identified from using a programmable robot in reception classes through to planning routes using a mapping CD-ROM in Year 6?

SCAA produced a non-statutory document *Planning the Curriculum at Key Stages 1 and 2*. It gives a range of recommendations and begins by placing your planning decisions in a whole school context. 'Planning . . . should be placed within the broader context of schools' overall curricular aims and policies' (SCAA, 1995b). If you do decide that some parts of the geography curriculum will be linked with other subjects, look to see that this is referred to in the school's aims, objectives and policies. Another example might be in fieldwork. If the geography, science and history policies clearly refer to structured fieldwork experiences, the school's whole school policy should reflect this. If you are gradually changing the ways in which subjects are linked and taught, check that this is clear in the school's development plans.

This document includes a paragraph needing careful study

❝ *We have made no assumptions about the merits or deficiencies of different approaches to the organisation of the primary curriculum. When working through the process, schools will need to decide, for example, which aspects of the curriculum are best suited to single subject teaching and which should be combined. However, these decisions should not be based on a general, unchallenged adherence to a single approach, but should take account of a range of considerations, including the nature of the various aspects of the curriculum, the teaching techniques and classroom organisation used, teachers' subject knowledge and expertise and the resources available.*
(SCAA, 1995b)

What does this mean for the geography coordinator?

- You may have inherited staff who have developed ways of teaching particular subjects. If they have always taught geography as part of an integrated topic, some INSET activites may be appropriate to ensure that they also have the skills and knowledge to teach it sometimes as a single subject.

- Look at the teaching spaces in your school. They will offer advantages and constraints for various teaching methods. If you have very large Key Stage 2 classes in small classrooms, it may affect the use of large map resources.

- If your budget limits your resources, it may be more effective to develop some teacher-led single subject lessons to ensure that the Programmes of Study are covered.

Think about the above paragraph in relation to your own school and note your ideas.

Many schools now think in terms of continuing and blocked units of work. This does have implications for geography and the linking of subjects. In the past topics or project work were often planned as blocked work. It may be worth looking at your whole school planning to decide whether this is still appropriate for all of geography. What parts of the geography curriculum could usefully be built into continuing units of work? For instance, children's understanding of weather may be more effectively developed by planning learning experiences to allow for systematic and gradual growth in their knowledge and understanding of seasonal changes and patterns. This often uses mathematical skills to collect, record and analyse data. Rather than building in constant weather topics, can some of the mathematics programmes of study, which incidentally will probably be taught as continuing units of work, be used to ensure experience of changing weather patterns.

Much geography will be planned as blocked work. SCAA (1995b) suggests that

Units can be linked when:

1   They contain common or complementary knowledge, understanding and skills;

2   The skills acquired in one subject or aspect of the curriculum can be applied or consolidated in the context of another;

3   The work in one subject or aspect of the curriculum provides a useful stimulus for work in another.   (SCAA, 1995b)

They also stress it is important to:

keep work focused by restricting the number of subjects or other aspects of the curriculum to be linked;

avoid contrived or artificial links between subjects or other aspects of the curriculum;

review the allocation of blocks of work to year groups to facilitate links being made, ensuring that this does not disturb subject progression.   (SCAA, 1995b)

> *blocked work is drawn, in the first instance, from a subject or aspect of the curriculum* [and that] *curriculum coherence can be strengthened by linking together, where appropriate, units of work from different subjects or aspects of the curriculum.*

As a coordinator, how might you justify such linking to staff and parents? When you have noted your ideas, compare then with the list offered by SCAA and think about how some of these might be relevant in your school.

Guidance has been developed specifically for geography (SCAA, 1997a) where they reinforce the view that *it is up to you to decide on an appropriate balance* between blocked, linked and continuing units of geographical work. Encouragingly, they also confirm ways in which geography can contribute to personal and social education and the whole curriculum:

> *Geographical fieldwork and investigations provide important opportunities for working in teams, developing individual responsibility and, on occasions, undertaking residential experience away from home.*
>
> *Because of its focus on places and environments in different parts of the world, and on issues which arise about how these are changing, geography provides a unique vehicle for environmental education, citizenship and learning about other cultures.*
> (SCAA, 1997a)

It will be interesting to keep the above references in mind when the post-Dearing review takes place. Will geography maintain its ground in the primary curriculum in the twenty-first century? To some extent you can influence that decision. Inspection evidence is being collected all the time, so if it can be shown that high quality planning, teaching and evaluation of the subject are taking place, it will strengthen the argument for at least retaining its current position in the curriculum. Chambers and Donert (1996) put this in perspective when they note that as a subject 'in some countries (such as the USA) it barely exists'.

With that sobering thought in mind we will turn to look at how geography may help to secure its place in the whole curriculum through making relevant links with other subjects and as a result, create a more unified and coherent set of learning experiences for your pupils. This brief list of ideas is intended to start you thinking about what may be possible in your school. It might also be a starting point for discussions with other colleagues as opportunities arise to make adaptations to your whole school planning.

Links with other subjects

English

A key focus here might be to look at your school planning. When teachers are working on their medium and short term planning what thought do they give to how geographical activities can use various parts of the English Orders? Some examples based on the Orders might include:

- sharing ideas and insights and opinions about an aerial photograph of the school;
- listening to other opinions and accounts of distant places;
- consideration of groups of words such as 'the hierarchy of settlement', words going from farm, hamlet, village through to city;
- use texts drawn from a variety of cultures and traditions;
- present a neat, correct and clear final copy of their geographical enquiry.

Much geographical work can offer interesting and relevant ways of covering the requirement of the English Orders with both subjects mutually reinforcing each other's aims. The booklet *Use of Language: a common approach* (SCAA, 1997e) gives further ideas for planning the use of language across the whole school curriculum. As a coordinator you need to be aware of such documents and make use of them as appropriate to your school.

Also, a practical source of ideas to offer staff can be found in the regular 'Inside Story' series in *Primary Geographer*. In each edition one children's book is discussed from a geographical point of view. Colleagues may find this an interesting way of building geography into their school day.

Mathematics

A range of mathematical skills have to be covered if the geography Orders are taught in full. A brief list includes

- coordinates and grid references
- scale
- angles and bearings
- proportion, shape and size
- classifying, representing and interpreting data through purposeful enquiries

Note the phrase 'purposeful enquiries' and consider its links with the geography Orders and enquiry processes.

Mathematics is normally planned and taught as continuous units owing to the subject nature. Quite often a structured scheme of teaching materials is used. Many things listed above will feature in this scheme. It may be worth discussing this with the mathematics coordinator to see how effective progress and continuity are between the geography and mathematics curriculum. For instance, where are coordinates taught in the mathematics scheme? How does this connect with the planned teaching of skills within the geography curriculum? You may be able to think of many similar questions to ask in your school.

Science

Geography and science share both techniques of enquiry and relevant links between content, for instance, protecting the environment. Many useful links can be established but the danger is that they dominate the curriculum and the distinctive nature of each subject is lost. As Chambers and Donert (1996) explain 'a major distinction between science and geography can be recognised in terms of the spatial and human elements in geography which are not central to science'. Your task with science will be to look at the whole curriculum and agree a balance of learning opportunities which will help pupils increase their understanding and interpretation of the world.

Information technology

Appropriate links are required by the Order. Geography provides many opportunities to use information technology in its fullest sense. In addition to computers, IT can mean

programmable robots	~ planning routes for a classroom post delivery buggy
e-mail	~ sending messages between your school and the school in your contrasting locality
videos (using and making)	~ groups of children making short videos to express ideas about the quality of their local environment
CD-ROMs	~ developing a line of enquiry through researching a CD-ROM atlas
fax messages	~ keeping in touch with your partner school in Europe
teletext information	~ searching for holiday information about your distant locality
world wide web	~ getting the latest information worldwide e.g. on a recent volcanic explosion
computer controlled weather station	~ collecting and analysing weather data over a long period
data loggers	~ measuring water temperature at points along the local stream
satellite remote sensing	~ discussing how information technology is applied in making satellite images and how they can give information, e.g. how the rainforest is changing

A helpful booklet (Geographical Association/National Council for Educational Technology, 1995) is available giving more ideas on developing IT skills and capability through geography.

This lists intentionally ends here. It is not because relevant links cannot be made with history, music and other subjects. Many can be established and as a primary teacher you will no doubt be able to identify them, but there is a danger that the process begins to resemble the now dated method of planning through topic webs where everything becomes related to everything else, however tenuous. 'This style of planning does not ensure continuity or progression, does not address processes, and is generally too broad to allow for depth of study' (Martin, 1995). Your coordinator's role requires that you can move beyond a class teacher's perspective on planning and look at the whole curriculum. What will work well in your school? How can you interpret the many official confirmations given in SCAA quotations in this chapter which support relevant links? An effective coordinator helps to create

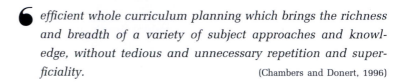

efficient whole curriculum planning which brings the richness and breadth of a variety of subject approaches and knowledge, without tedious and unnecessary repetition and superficiality.
(Chambers and Donert, 1996)

Chapter 7

What the coordinator needs to know about fieldwork and the law

> ❝ *More opportunities should be taken for investigative work and fieldwork in the school grounds and locally, as well as further afield.*
>
> (OFSTED, 1995c)

This chapter looks at the role you will play in coordinating fieldwork activities throughout the school. It discusses key legal issues related to your work. It also gives a number of references to other sources which provide detailed information on various topics, for instance developing enquiry approaches through fieldwork.

The timetable is very crowded and money scarce in most primary schools. How can you justify fieldwork? Spend a few minutes jotting down the reasons you would give if someone challenged you about why fieldwork should be a part of the curriculum. As you do this consider:

■ your school context — children and their experiences
resources
stated philosophy, aims and objectives;
■ what you personally believe to be important;
■ what you know about official statements.

When you have done this look at the following questions and see how they relate to your ideas.
■ Does it help children to work with real people, places, events and issues?

- Are geographical skills, knowledge and understanding developed?
- Can it be used to aid geographical enquiry?
- Can personal and social skills grow through fieldwork experiences?
- Is it enjoyable?
- Will children's awareness of environmental issues be raised?
- Are experiences provided which cannot be given in the classroom?
- Does it involve people in the wider community?
- Is fieldwork an integral part of whole school curriculum planning?

Using these questions and your ideas, you may begin to form an outline for the aims of your fieldwork policy. Its justification will be embedded in the needs of your school and set in a broader context. A complete geography policy will include a fieldwork policy within it, however, check with your headteacher to see if the school has an agreed way of setting out such policies to provide consistency and ease of use by staff. Also, talk to them about where your fieldwork policy should be included. While it will probably be a part of the geography policy, they may also wish to integrate it within the school's health and safety policies. Whatever is decided, the policy should be consistent. It should be clear, short, helpful and understandable by everyone who needs to be aware of it, for instance, parent helpers and volunteers.

A school fieldwork policy should include:

- school fieldwork philosophy
- aims and objectives
- curriculum map showing where fieldwork is planned into the whole curriculum
- fieldwork planning grids and check lists
- outlines of what these experiences include — locations
  - aims
  - activities
  - teaching and learning styles
  - resources
  - intended outcomes
- clarification about opportunities for flexibility and innovation within the agreed plans
- special needs/equal opportunities statement

Some schools also create an on-going file of fieldtrip reports. These tend to be for whole days and longer visits. They can be based on a simple proforma and include space for the leader to briefly comment on what they found and did. For instance, remarks might include:

parts of the Roman fort will be closed for two years owing to an excavation;

there are new toilet facilities near the car park;

the next person who takes a group should ask for Christine to be their guide — she's excellent at getting the children to ask questions about the buildings;

a swimming pool opens at the residential centre next year — remember to ask parents to pack swimming things for next visit.

- health and safety policy
- copies of up-to-date school paperwork e.g. letters to parents, policy on payment for visits
- equipment and resources list including locations of items
- other relevant school information e.g. preferred coach company, current list of parents willing to act as helpers.

Although it probably would not be included within a policy document, can you begin to build up a record of what happens on the various field visits? This could be based on

- sets of photographs,
- folders of children's work,
- a video of a residential study visit,
- photographs of an assembly or display describing it —

and may also become part of your coordinator's portfolio. They can serve a number of purposes:

- an interesting and enjoyable record of school events,
- helpful information for future visits,
- a record of work which you can show OFSTED and other visitors which they might not otherwise be able to experience.

Realistically, when you take on the coordinator's role there will be a number of things to find out. A lot of it might arise from the work you do on developing the fieldwork policy. Each school will be different, but the examples below have been chosen to sharpen your thinking and initiative about the job you have to do in your situation. As you read the next section, note ways in which the points apply to your school and jot down your own ideas. Another way to use this section is to make a personal action plan but if you do this keep it simple and prioritise the order in which you think things need to be done.

What fieldwork actually happens at the moment? How can I find out?
It may not be included in planning papers and schemes of work so you will need to talk to people as well as using these documents.

What policies already exist? Where are they? How do they fit into whole school policies? Is anyone actually using them?
Don't start your own writing until you have a picture of this. It might affect what you write. For instance, you may discover that no enquiry work happens on visits: it's all filling in simple worksheets. This will influence what your short term goals might be and what you want to make clear in any paperwork and INSET activities.

Why does fieldwork happen as it does?

Don't always assume the worst! The visit to the secretary's family farm might be very worthwhile. Go along if you can. If you can't, talk to the children and adult helpers when they return. Keep your eyes open before and after a class or year group go on a visit to see what preparatory and followup work is done. A really interesting corridor display could give you the chance to tell the teacher how effective it is.

When is fieldwork carried out?

Some schools never plan winter outings because of the weather! Others take Year 6 out only in the summer term when SATs are over. Is this really making the best use of the opportunities? Can you convince staff that there may be a better way?

What role do adult helpers play on visits?

Some are no more than guard dogs and in certain situations this might be important. The most effective use of adults is made when they really know why the trip is happening. Can you encourage colleagues to spent a short time talking to helpers about the aims of the visit? Perhaps it's to get Year 3 children to really look closely at what people are selling in the local market. Are there key geographical words which helpers might use regularly during the day? What questions can help children develop geographical skills?

What resources are used and how?

This question may highlight the need for more equipment. You may find that a visit to a local river with clipboard questions is a result of not having anything to actually develop enquiries with. Or it could be because teachers are still using resources made long before National Curriculum developments. They may be satisfied because they have actually made it to the river. You then have a very tactful role to play in moving their confidence forward.

Are a range of sites and localities used?

Within the guidelines of using the locality at Key Stages 1 and 2, where do they actually go? You need to find out how suitable the sites are for what happens there. This is where it's important for you to get to know the locality really well. Do the sites give opportunities for progress and continuity to take place? For instance, if you know that simple map making is done in Year 4, where does it develop during the Year 6 visits? Have people thought about what can be done particularly well in any given place? For instance, a river study provides many opportunities for posing questions and taking measurements to help answer them. A farm visit might develop different skills in interviewing people and mapping how the land is used.

Perhaps the most important questions to ask are about the learning and teaching styles used during any fieldwork. Booth et al. (1993) suggest a list of 32 terms describing fieldwork. Examples include 'cooks tour', 'field teaching', 'issue based', 'humanistic' and 'talk and gawk'. Your role as coordinator will be to monitor and develop a balanced range of learning and teaching experiences throughout the programme. Also, it will be helpful if you can focus particular styles on visits where they will be most effective. Chambers and Donert (1996) offer this list of factors which will help decide on the styles used:

1   The knowledge, intuition and experience of the teacher.
2   The nature, commitment, personality and experience of the pupils.
3   The demands of the National Curriculum.
4   The nature of the fieldwork location.
5   The aims and balance of the fieldwork.
6   The educational philosophy of the individual teacher and the school.

It is likely that individual teachers will be planning and leading the fieldwork experiences for their own classes. You will not be able to influence teaching and learning styles of every visit, but a useful way to start might be to identify staff who are interested in developing their fieldwork strategies. Offer to help with the planning and resourcing of a visit. If you find that they are thinking of running the trip as a lecture because they can't find enough helpers to arrange more investigative groupwork, can you find more helpers for them? If you offer support and the trip is successful and enjoyable, you will probably have a colleague ready to support other ideas you might like to develop.

Another aspect of your work will be providing support in the planning and practical arrangements for field visits. Much of this will be steered by the methods used in your school. If you do need ideas on detailed planning and how the practicalities of fieldwork are managed, they can be found in the *Fieldwork in Action* (May et al. 1993–1996) series of books published by the Geographical Association.

Some legal considerations

A section with such a title might put teachers off for life in ever wanting to develop fieldwork activities. It need not be so. Your prime consideration must be the safety and welfare of the children and the adults who accompany them. Any help or guidelines you provide must be closely linked with the whole school health and safety policy. The following questions might be used as a part of your action plan. No list can include everything needed in all schools. Use it as an *aide memoire* and a sounding board for asking the questions relevant to your school.

Are you familiar with the school and LEA health and safety policies, especially those sections regarding fieldwork?

Have you discussed them with the head and agreed a framework for development?

Are you clear about the school's policy regarding parental permission and the payment for visits at any scale and location?

Do you and all your colleagues have some form of professional insurance and understand the nature of it?

You will be making the most of your fieldwork:

If it introduces children to a range of new places, people, issues and knowledge;

If it helps them to start asking questions about the physical and human processes and patterns they see in the world;

If they can begin to understand environmental relationships and issues;

If they have opportunities to begin to understand their role as citizens;

and finally, if they actually enjoy exploring and experiencing new places and meeting new people.

Does everyone know and follow the regulations on transport? For instance, supervision on coaches and the use of personal transport to carry pupils.

Is there a school system for checking the trustworthiness of helpers, especially important on residential visits?

Are you aware of the implications of the access requirements in the geography Order to ensure they are applied in fieldwork as well as classroom activities?

Do you understand how pupils' health issues are covered? For instance, the administration of medicine on a residential visit or diet and allergy requirements of particular pupils.

Do you know and understand the 1974 Health and Safety at Work Act which applies when you organise and run activities not held in licensed centres? These centres are covered by The Activity Centres (Young Persons' Safety) Act 1995 and The Adventure Activities Licensing Regulations 1996. The DfE Circular 22/94 also explains how to carry out a risk assessment exercise and why it should be done. The headteacher should be familiar with these documents and will probably be willing to talk to you about them if this is new territory for you.

These are serious issues and it may perhaps be good to end this chapter by returning to some of the fundamental reasons for studying the world beyond the classroom. All children come to school with very different experiences of the world. These will affect the range of fieldwork activities you plan. For some, a walk around a nearby lake will be a big adventure and you may well have as many personal and social reasons for doing it as geographical ones. For others who regularly travel the world with their parents sealed in cars and planes, a day walking in a remote and hilly place in your contrasting locality may be physically challenging and exhilarating.

Part three Whole school policies and schemes of work

Chapter 8

Preparing for a whole school policy
for geography

> The success of a policy is visible, tangible evidence of it in
> practice in everyday school life . . . not a folder gathering dust
> on a shelf.
> (Foley and Janikoun, 1996)

Developing a whole school policy for geography will be one
of your main activities as a coordinator. The first section of
this chapter examines why it is necessary to have a policy.
The second section discusses a range of processes you may
use to develop a policy in your school.

Why have a geography policy?

It may be worth starting this discussion by standing back
and taking a broad look at what a policy can actually do
in your school. One of the key skills for any coordinator is
this ability to take in the wider picture beyond their own
classroom, not only within the school but further afield. A
successful policy can work in two ways:

1 it acts as a public statement of the school's intentions for
   children's learning in geography and how these will be
   achieved;

2 its creation and development provide a focus for everyone
   working on it to examine what is happening and to take
   ownership of the decisions stated in it.

It is possible for you go away and write a policy and present it to the staff. But doing this can remove the opportunity to see policy development as a set of useful processes within your school. These include:

- valuing the ideas and experience of other staff;
- giving them ownership of the decisions;
- providing the opportunity to examine and discuss their own practice in teaching geography.

If you can develop a policy through involving colleagues as much as possible you may achieve more active use of it in practice. Clearly, this is going to depend on the ethos of your school. If all other policies have been devised by subject coordinators and presented to staff you may only be able to take these ideas so far and forcing the issue could leave you with even less support. This is where it may be useful talking to the headteacher before you do any work on policy development. It may even be that they are looking for a way of getting such activities going in the school.

Even if you can only involve other staff in some parts of the development process, the policy has to be unique to your school and its current stage of development. Your policy will change over time. Indeed you may be in a school where there is a timetable in the development plan for the review of each subject's policy. Again, this may be something to discuss with the headteacher, because a working policy has to fit the needs of your school and this book cannot provide an off-the-shelf policy to use in a particular school. It can provide ideas on the framework for a policy and that is covered in Chapter 9.

There may be the temptation to use a policy from another school or published source, but trying to adapt one of these to your school often takes more time and energy than using a framework on which to build your own. Each policy has a particular feel and style and this often reflects the school ethos. Inspectors can quickly sense whether a policy has been developed within the school or adapted from other sources!

Policy development will take time, but there are a number of reasons why the process and outcome are important. A well designed policy with useful content will be used by the staff. They will actually find it helpful. At one level they may find the aims stated in it can help to clarify their reasons for particular lesson plans. At another level, it may contain a list of booklets to which they can refer for guidance. You can use this idea as one process in assessing the success of your work. Look around the school and see if the geography policy is being used. Ask people when and how they use it. The information you collect may guide some changes in the future.

Another important function of a policy is that it gives useful information to teachers, governors, parents, inspectors and other people involved in the school. This is an important point to remember when you are designing its structure and writing it. Presentation needs to be clear and simple. Keep it as short as possible. Don't use jargon. A readable policy will strengthen your case for the subject. With the relatively low status of geography at the present time, this is especially important for you.

An effective policy will clarify how the broad aims and values of the school are reflected in a particular subject, providing clear information about how these are put into practice. Each subject has particular ways in which it can support the wider aims of the school and it may be that in your discussions on policy development you can identify some of these and ensure they have prominence. For instance, if one of your school's aims is to promote the involvement of the wider community in children's learning, this can be reinforced in your policy's section on locality studies and the people who might be asked to work with the pupils on their enquiries. Become familiar with the key policy documents in your school and begin to see how their statements may be relevant in the geography policy.

Teachers will be able to use a well-designed geography policy in their planning work. It will remind them clearly of what the main aims are. It might include a scheme of work which explains how their work fits into a broader picture: this can enhance progress and continuity. It should inform them about available resources and ways of using them and provide a first stop for finding practical information, for instance, any health and safety issues for fieldwork.

Teachers are the central audience for the policy but an effective coordinator will be aware of the needs of other audiences and the potential of the policy to create change and development. Geography resources are an example of this. If you can clearly explain what current resources are used for and the rationale for your purchasing programme, you will give governors and other people a clear and professional picture about why money needs to be allocated to the subject within a particular programme of development. You cannot do everything at once, an important fact to bear in mind at inspection times. If your policy is clear about where you are now and has realistic plans for the future, you will be in a stronger position to discuss them. It shows that you have ideas and a picture of where you are going. If this information can be tracked to other documents such as the school development plan, minutes of governors' meetings and your coordinator's portfolio, your case will be even stronger.

A geography policy also provides a mirror through which to reflect progress. It should contain information and ideas about how the subject will develop and a broad timetable of action. One example might be to ensure that an INSET programme takes place in order to build the personal confidence of the staff for teaching geography. Another might be the gradual development of a series of fieldwork experiences across the whole age range in your school. Again, if this has been discussed with staff there is more likelihood of success if they feel they have some ownership of the decisions which have been made and written into the policy.

Perhaps one of the most important reasons for developing a policy centres around the children themselves. As teachers we manage a set of learning experiences over the time they are in our school and they internalise many messages from how we organise them. A coherent policy can help teachers but it should also be flexible to ensure these experiences are relevant to the children. This is particularly so in geography because you are not working with a tightly prescribed set of content in the Orders and you are in control of the localities in which to work. If your policy can provide colleagues with the confidence to make informed decisions about the details in their planning, it will be successful. This is perhaps summed up clearly by Alexander, Willcocks, Kinder and Nelson (1995) when they talk about planning which is secured by teachers. They argue that this approach

> does not dictate precisely the form of action, but it ensures that one thinks through possibilities and contingencies and provides a resource upon which one can draw if necessary.

An effective geography policy provides information, ideas and a clear structure on which everyone working with the children can draw in order to help them begin to understand the fascinating range of people and places around the world. Perhaps most of all it should capture some of the excitement and challenge of the explorations in which they can take part.

Developing a whole school policy for geography

This is seen by coordinators in many curriculum subjects as one of the biggest jobs they have to do. One way of tackling it is to break the job down into a series of smaller steps. This section suggests a number of steps that you might take. Do bear in mind that each school is unique and one of your skills as a successful coordinator is to decide both the precise order which will work in your school and the level of emphasis each stage will need. To give a practical example, it may be that you have taken over the role from someone who developed a very appropriate geography scheme of work, but you find it is not used because there are very few resources and, although willing, staff do not understand the opportunities it provides for their planning. That will be a very different situation from one where the scheme of work is inappropriate and the whole subject has a very low profile in the school. So, when you start work on your policy development accept that things will take time and be prepared to be flexible: you will discover many things along the way which you were not expecting!

What is happening now?

We discussed the use of a personal portfolio in Chapter 2. The information you collect and your ideas on planning should all be kept in it, both to make life easier for you and to act as a source of information for anyone wanting to see how your thinking and action are progressing. The information could be stored:

in a notebook;

in a personal diary;

as a collection of documents.

You will need to collect information from many places. As you read the list below think about where you may find some of the answers to these questions in your own school.

- What does the present policy say and how much of it is actually happening?

- What geography are the children actually doing?

- How is this geography being taught?

- What resources are available, how are they used, where are they stored and how easy are they to get at?

- Where is geography taught well in your school and where is there scope for development?

- What are people thinking and saying about geography? This may be an important question depending on the leadership style of the previous geography coordinator.

- What do other school documents say about areas relevant to geography?

- How much do people understand about geography? The perceptions of governors, parents and teachers will vary a great deal.

- Are you aware of the many other sources of influence? The DfEE, SCAA, OFSTED, local advisers, curriculum and teachers' centres, local universities and the local community may all have valuable sources of information and help to assist you in developing a policy.

- What ideas does the headteacher have and what levels of management support are you likely to get?

- Are there any other coordinators who have valuable experience of developing a policy in your school? How might they be able to help you and are there ways in which your subject interests could mutually support each other?

There may be other questions which you will want to add to the list.

Building an action plan

As you ask these questions some patterns may begin to emerge and priorities become clearer.

The next stage is to think about your short, medium and longer term aims. This need not be rigid and may change as new information or opportunities arise. For instance, a change in governors' budgeting plans may give you money for resources earlier than you expected: this may allow you to begin some initiative which had been given a long term priority. Be flexible and alert to new opportunities to make geography a real focus of activity! All of this work will give you a clearer idea of where the school is at the moment.

This is now the time to think about where you want geography to go in the longer term. Your ideas on this will come from:
- your personal definition of what geographical education is in the primary school;
- the current legal framework;
- ideas, information and values put forward in INSET, journals, TV programmes and other sources.

Your action plan is one way of getting from where you are now to the more long term goals.

Share the ideas in your action plan with the head and staff. Ask them for their ideas and opinions in an attempt to give them ownership even at this early stage.

Discussing the possibilities

As well as these informal discussions with staff, it may now be appropriate to set up a series of discussions or meetings to look at some initial ideas. One approach is to prepare a draft statement explaining the overall aims for geography. This is then discussed with the staff, revised to take account of their corporate ideas and acts as a basis for further work. If you feel that the staff would prefer a more open-ended approach and can manage the process, that could be another way forward.

These early discussions could also focus on building a set of desired outcomes which are agreed by the staff. These can naturally build into an early version of the school policy and become integrated within your action plan. This has the advantage of perhaps combining both your vision for geography along with the ideas of other people into an agreed way forward. The following statements are examples of some things you may all agree to develop:

- to review the current topic headings in the whole school's plans for their suitability as vehicles for teaching geography;

- to assess the opportunities for developing IT in geographical work;

- to clarify the role of cross-curricular issues in geographical work;

- to develop a programme of fieldwork activities which promote progression and continuity in the learning of geographical skills and enquiries;

- to create an INSET programme to extend the geographical understanding of members of staff;

- to bring together all the geography resources, look at their suitability and devise new ways and means of storage and access.

If you have already begun to audit geography in your school, you may now be able to begin to write your own list of possible statements for action.

As you develop your policy it is important to remember that anything which has been agreed for inclusion should be feasible in your situation. There is no point in making statements which are unlikely to be seen in practice. Don't be afraid to begin in a small way and adapt the wording in the policy as you make progress. For instance, rather than saying that information technology is used in all appropriate geography lessons, it may be better for your first version of a policy to state that 'information technology will be used in appropriate lessons for collecting, representing and interpreting data'. If a cross-reference can appear in the mathematics policy and it actually happens in the classroom, then you are beginning to create a policy which is making a difference to teaching and learning.

Another important part of the process of developing a geography policy will be in the design of a scheme of work. You will need to be realistic here. You may have studied the current scheme of work and whole school planning and decided that a number of major changes need to take place. But even a less than adequate scheme of work can have complex connections across the curriculum. Changes in one place can have a knock-on effect in others.

For instance, you may feel that giving a whole half term to every geography-focused topic is not an ideal way of working. Any changes will need careful discussion and management with many interested parties. This may mean breaking into a two year cycle of planned work. Having looked at all these implications, don't give up! Rather, see if there are ways of making some small scale changes in areas where you judge there could be a good chance of success.

When colleagues see the results of your ideas it may then be possible to widen your targets. Success tends to build on success. You may only have one chance to get it right in order to retain your credibility. We will look at issues relating to geography schemes of work in more depth in Chapter 10. Before that, Chapter 9 will discuss what a prototype geography policy might contain and how it may be adapted to the needs of your school.

Creating your school geography policy

> The geography policy underpins the teaching of geography throughout the school. It is not a scheme of work: the policy gives the why? where? when? of the geography curriculum.
>
> (Richardson, 1995)

In the previous chapter we looked at the various processes you might use to build a geography policy. At some point you will have to commit yourself to paper and it would be wise to discuss it first with your headteacher to decide which approach is suitable for your school.

Some schools now have a format and list of headings which are used by all subjects. If this is so in your school, you will have to follow this method. Read existing policies carefully. Are they really clear? Is the structure helpful? How might you use the given structure to make some points you believe are specific to geography? If the resources exist in your LEA, consult advisers and advisory teachers about suggestions and support they may be able to offer. This can be especially helpful if your school is preparing for an OFSTED inspection. Advisers will often be very willing to look through your geography policy and other documents and offer critical and constructive advice.

If you are able to create your own structure and headings, again, see how other subjects have approached the activity. Which ideas could you adapt and use in your policy?

Remember that a policy needs to be easily understood and *used* by busy teachers, governors, parents and other readers such as OFSTED inspectors. All these audiences need to understand your message. Avoid jargon.

Various writers and advisory groups offer lists of headings which can be used to create a policy document. From such lists each school needs to decide:

- which ones are appropriate for their situation;
- what will be included under each heading;
- the emphasis given to each section;
- the overall style of the document.

Richardson's (1995) checklist of 'what you might usefully include in a geography policy' is a helpful starting point:

1   An attractive cover — an opportunity to use a geography logo

2   Aims and objectives

3   What does National Curriculum geography look like/how is it organised/what does a key stage plan look like?

4   Where does geography occur in the school?

5   Teaching and learning styles — are these related to the school policy?

6   Progression

7   Differentiation

8   Special needs

9   Fieldwork

10   Information Technology

11   Resources: artefacts, books, photographs, videos, slides, human resoures.

12   Assessment, recording and record keeping

13   Evaluation of work done: from teacher's point of view and pupil's point of view.

The following topics may be added to this list:

- a statement explaining how the policy was developed, where geography is now and where it hopes to go in the future;

- description of how the policy will be reviewed;

- a statement describing the school locality and context — this can give precise information to justify much of your locality work both near and far.

- brief reference to appropriate evidence from your coordinator's portfolio.

There can be a temptation to put too much into a policy document. Keep it simple and concise and make clear reference to other relevant materials. In this way you should end up with a number of documents available for scrutiny:

> An accurate and informative policy document;
>
> A scheme of work covering the whole school;
>
> Your coordinator's portfolio;
>
> A job description for the geography coordinator.

Together, these will provide a complete picture of where the current state of geography has come from, what is happening now and where you are planning to go in the future.

The actual process of creating the policy can vary between schools and the methods you have used to engage colleagues in the process. You may find that you are expected to write sections, take them to meetings for discussion and gradually build up the policy in stages. Alternatively, after initial discussions you could be expected to go away and complete the task, then perhaps it will be agreed at a staff meeting where only minor changes are discussed and agreed. Whatever system is used the policy will at some stage have to be approved by senior management in the school and the governing body.

Each policy has to be unique to the school in which it is used. The policy set out below is provided to give an example of how one school has taken key headings and filled them out with details unique to their situation and may provide ideas for a starting point for developing your own policy. It may also be a catalyst for staff discussion in your school. As you become familiar with it, you will begin to understand the unique feel which geography has in this particular school. Again, this reinforces the point that you cannot take a policy from another school and use it in your own. It is reproduced with grateful thanks to the headteacher and staff of Newtown Infant School, Stockton on Tees. The background to the development of the policy was described by the headteacher in this way:

> *Although documentation of this nature is not written purely to satisfy OFSTED, schools would be irresponsible to ignore what the Framework for Inspection says about geography.*
>
> *We decided that the geography policy, along with all other curriculum policies, should be a broad set of intentions which state the aspirations and aims for the subject in our school. All subject policies written for Newtown Infant School conform to the same headings. This is a deliberate decision in order to create uniformity across the school.*

This chapter has been included in order to be a focus for you to do some practical work on beginning to decide what your policy may contain. Keep the following questions in mind as you study the policy developed at Newtown Infant School and maybe use them to begin to make notes which you can use when writing or adapting your school policy:

■ What headings will describe most accurately the geography in my school?

■ What will I include under each heading?

■ How much detail will I go into?

■ What writing style will be most appropriate for the various audiences?

■ In what ways will the style reflect the prevailing ethos and values of our school?

■ What will the overall presentation of the policy look like?

Newtown Infant School

Policy for Geography

- This document is a statement of the aims, principles and strategies for teaching and learning of geography at Newtown Infant School.
- It was developed during the spring of 1995 through a process of consultation with teaching staff.
- It was approved by the governing body during 1995.
- This policy will be reviewed in 1998.

What is geography?

Geography is the exploration and understanding of the childrens' surroundings and the world in which we live.

Aims

Our aims in teaching geography are that all children will:

- enjoy studying the world around them;
- develop their knowledge and understanding of places in local, regional, national, international and global contexts;
- develop knowledge and understanding of the physical elements of geography, including weather and climate, water forms, landforms, animal and plant life;
- develop their knowledge and understanding of human geography looking at populations, settlements and communications;
- understand the world and the part natural resources play, and the possibilities of protecting and managing environments;
- develop an awareness of the environment and environmental issues within it;
- develop practical skills in the use of resources (maps, atlases, compasses) and the ability to apply these skills when applicable with confidence and understanding;
- stimulate their enquiring minds.

Principles of the teaching and learning of geography

Geography is important because

- it is a body of knowledge essential to our understanding of the world around us and making sense of the world around us;
- it is interesting and enjoyable, providing an awareness of other places and peoples;
- the skills and knowledge of geography have wide applicability in everyday life.

Geography is a foundation subject in the National Curriculum. The fundamental skills, knowledge and concepts of the subject are set out in 'Key Stages 1 and 2 of the National Curriculum' where they are categorised into a single attainment target called geography.

Strategies for the teaching of geography

The geography curriculum is organised on a topic basis wherein geography is integrated into the yearly programme of topics followed throughout the school.

In addition to this integrated geography programme the following extra activities are carried out:

1 carrying out tasks asked in assemblies;
2 using resources permanently displayed in the classrooms;
3 using areas set up within classrooms offering geographical experiences e.g. travel agencies, geography areas, weather stations, hospitals, shops;
4 environmental activities pursued e.g. gardening club, caring for wildlife gardens within school grounds, litter picking, tree, bulb and flower planting in and outside school;
5 being involved in projects organised by outside agencies e.g. BTCV, Cleveland Wildlife Trust, *Evening Gazette*.

The predonimant mode of working in geography is groupwork although individual work and class teaching are used where appropriate. Within this structure:

- groups are usually of mixed ability with differentiation by role;
- teacher produced workcards are frequently used;
- relevant discussion is encouraged;
- groups are encouraged to communicate findings in a variety of ways
- **There is no specialist teaching in geography**, it is taught by class teachers
- **Classroom helpers are used in geography** to assist in:
    supporting group activities
    providing extra help for children with particular needs

to read stories with geographical content

to maintain good care and condition of geographical resources

to accompany and supervise groups in outside activities

on outings and visits by fostering discussion and questioning among small groups

- **Commercially available packs** are used to support topic work and geographical themes. The principal packs in use in the school are: Oliver and Boyd
  Key Start

- **Pupils with special needs** have the same geography entitlement as all other pupils and are offered the same curriculum

- **Homework** is used to support geography through tasks such as:

  finding answers to questions posed in school through the use of books, atlases and interviews with friends and family

  finding and bringing in artefacts and resources from outside school

  sending postcards to school when on holiday

- **The emphasis in our teaching of geography** is on stimulating the children's enquiring minds and satisfying their growing need to 'know the reason why'

- whenever possible make geography real to the children by offering opportunities for direct experience, practical activities and exploration

- resources are made readily available and accessible

- **Excellence in geography is celebrated** in display and performance including:

  the mounting of children's work, be it individual pieces, group offerings or whole class efforts around the school

  feedback by children to rest of class both orally and visually

  class and whole school assemblies showing a celebration of class topic work

  individual or group performance highlighting activities of a geographical nature

  showing other classes samples of work

  showing headteacher samples of excellent work

Strategies for ensuring progress and continuity

Planning in geography is a process in which all teachers are involved, wherein

- the foundation for curricular planning is the whole school development plan
- a cycle of topic plans is drawn up by staff working groups and is carefully balanced to ensure full coverage of the National Curriculum
- schemes of work for geography are developed by the coordinator (in collaboration with the whole staff)
- medium plans are drawn up by teachers in year group teams for each half term and are monitored by the team leader and the headteacher
- daily lesson plans ae written by individual teachers

The role of the geography coordinator is to

- take the lead in policy development and the production of schemes of work designed to ensure progression and continuity in geography throughout the school
- support colleagues in this development of detailed work plans, their implementation of the scheme of work and in assessment and record keeping activities
- monitor progress in geography and advise the headteacher on action needed
- take responsibility for the purchase and organisation of central resources for geography
- keep up to date with developments in geography education and disseminate information to colleagues as appropriate

Feedback to pupils about their own progress in geography is usually done while a task is being carried out through discussion between child and teacher, and through the marking of work. Effective marking

- aims to be encouraging and supportive
- is often done while a task is being carried out, through discussion between child and teacher
- includes ticks and written comments which aim to be positive and constructive

Formative assessment is used to guide the progress of individual pupils in geography. It involves identifying each child's progress, determining what each child has learned and what therefore should be the next stage in his/her learning. Formative assessment is mostly carried out informally by teachers in the course of their teaching. Suitable tasks for assessment include

- small group discussions perhaps in the context of a practical task
- specific assignments for individual pupils
- individual discussions in which children are encouraged to appraise their own work and progress
- class circle activities where children offer suggestions and answers to teacher led tasks

Strategies for recording and reporting

Records of progress in geography kept for each child contain
- a yearly report of progress to parents through a written report
- a portfolio of work, dated and annotated with teacher comments and containing exceptional items of achievement and progress
- comments made in individual teacher's daily record books

Reporting to parents is done twice a year through interviews and annually through a written report. Exceptional work is brought to parents' notice when appropriate. Reporting in geography will focus on each child's
- attitude to geography
- competence in geographical skills
- ability to apply geographical skills and knowledge to new work
- progress in geography

Strategies for the use of resources

Classroom resources in geography include
- waxed playmats
- waxed maps
- commercial maps
- a variety of atlases
- a globe
- aerial photographs of school
- plans of the school and local area
- a variety of Playmobil
- a selection of construction apparatus e.g. Lego

Central resources in geography are the responsibility of the geography coordinator. They include
- sets of atlases
- children's reference books
- teachers' reference books
- geography based story books
- commercial packs
- pre-recorded video tapes of geography programmes and geographical topics
- selection of nationality dolls
- selection of teacher-made resources
- artefacts including costumes, wall-hangings, money from different countries
- cassettes
- a geography section in children's library within school
- aerial photographs

External resources include
- points of the compass painted on the playground
- a senses garden in main playground
- two inner courtyard wildlife areas
- local area

Information technology is a resource which is used in geography for
- written work
- illustrations
- handling information
- directional work

The library has a selection on geography which provides a substantial resource of reference materials for the whole school.

Health and safety issues in geography include
- wearing gloves when picking litter
- wearing gloves when gardening
- handling garden tools as taught
- being aware of school policy on using outside areas within school grounds for activities (see Appendix)
- being aware of school policy on visits and excursions to places within and outside the county (see Appendix)

The Newtown Infant School geography policy then includes the following documents in the appendices
1. Policy on fieldwork within the school grounds
2. Policy on school visits and excursions
3. List of centrally held resources
4. List of staff reference books

Hopefully, you will have not only gained a clear idea of how geography is taught but also begun to sense what is unique to that school. For instance, there is a clear message that using the school grounds is an important aspect of their work. Another one is the emphasis placed on children becoming actively engaged in geographical enquiry and reporting their findings in a variety of ways. Remember, that if such features are developed within your policy, it should be possible to track them for consistency in other school policy documents. For instance, the Newtown English policy might well have a reference to clear planning of language activities into various curriculum subjects. This will reinforce the ways in which whole school planning and issues are brought together into a set of coherent learning experiences for all children. It also illustrates how all members of staff need to work together whatever role they have in the school.

A policy document should state when it will next be reviewed and this date should also be referred to in the whole school development plan. Once the policy is up and running, use your personal portfolio to keep notes on aspects which might need changing when the review time comes around. This will make your task easier in two ways:
- you will not have to rely on memory for the many things which will have happened;
- it will provide evidence to support the possible need for changes.

You will monitor the policy in action and ideally other colleagues will support you in this. For instance, they may suggest that changes need to be made to records of pupil progress in geography as they are not always clear when children move to their next class. You may observe that while there are many geographical resources within the school grounds, teachers are perhaps not aware/confident in using them within their teaching. As Foley and Janikoun (1996) remind us 'the success of a policy is visible, tangible evidence of it in practice in everyday school life'. If you see this taking place, it is one indication of success in a major part of your role as geography coordinator.

Chapter 10

Planning the geography curriculum

> ❝ *Every school is different and will need to design a curriculum to meet its own particular circumstances.*   (SCAA, 1995b)

The planning process will involve you in a number of choices. On the one hand you have a personal set of values and beliefs developed through your experiences as a teacher. On the other hand society imposes a set of values, beliefs, laws and circumstances within which you have to make decisions. As Threlfall (1997) explains

> ❝ *As an educator, on whatever level, you have an exciting and problematical task: how can you best prepare your children for life within a constantly changing society and how can you effectively organise and plan the curriculum to that end?*

This chapter will examine aspects of the planning process through the eyes of a geography coordinator. A great deal has been written on planning: 'official' sources such as SCAA and OFSTED, and educational writers who either focus on education generally or a subject in particular to name but two sources. If you need practical ideas on basic planning methods for geography there are a number of useful starting points:

Plans for Primary Geography (Morgan, 1995) offers ideas for planning across Key Stages 1 and 2. Even these cannot be taken and used off the shelf by every school so you will need to adapt them to your needs.

Planning the Curriculum at Key Stages 1 and 2 (SCAA, 1995b) provides a variety of planning strategies. The suggestions on blocked and linked subjects are worth studying in order to decide on the collection of approaches suitable for your school. The fact that geography can be easily linked with science, history, mathematics, IT and English can be confusing when looking at whole school planning and this booklet provides some non-statutory guidance on a range of possibilities.

Geography at Key Stage 2. Curriculum Planning Guidance for Teachers (SCAA, 1997a) again is non-statutory. However, it provides very concise and practical advice on basic curriculum planning. It may be a document which you could use with colleagues who need some clear and non-threatening ideas to get them started with quality planning. Again, it is important to adapt the suggestions to your school.

These and other books are written for a wide range of readers. Reference will be made to a number of them, allowing you to use ideas and information from them.

The content of this chapter takes into account the particular circumstances in which you may find yourself as a subject coordinator. It could be based on all or some of these influences:

■ Many planning decisions have already been made in your school. If things are going to change effectively they need to be done from an informed perspective by a coordinator who has evidence and skills at their fingertips.

■ You are approaching this stage of the school's planning from a particular background. You may have been directly involved in earlier decision-making or perhaps you are new to your role/the school.

■ The Dearing curriculum is in full flow and a review is planned. You may well have the responsibility of leading any changes required by the five year review within the particular context of your school.

Unless you are working in a brand new school it is likely that planning decisions you will be involved in stem from a number of sources:

- perhaps the staff have agreed to review the units of work within a whole key stage;

- an OFSTED report requires that your action plan includes major revision of some schemes of work;

- your junior school has recently amalgamated with the feeder infant school and a detailed review of progress and continuity across the curriculum is required.

At this point, it may be worth considering what changes in planning are needed in your school and how they have arisen.

■ As a coordinator you have a responsibility to monitor and evaluate geography across the whole school. This requires that you can wear a particular set of 'spectacles' when thinking about planning. The view you see is much broader than that of a class teacher. Hopefully, you are beginning to make planning decisions by seeing them as an on-going process of change which the school constantly experiences.

The sub sections of this chapter provide both a resource through which to filter ideas and a set of perspectives on planning which examine issues with a particular focus on the needs of geography within your school. They are designed to act as a source of reference for the many types of planning in which you will be involved. The chapter does not contain detailed planning grids, schemes of work and other devices. Many examples of these can be found in LEA guidelines, Geographical Association publications and SCAA documents. The subsections here are written in order to help you assess the extent to which such materials may be useful and as a lens through which to examine your current planning processes and paperwork. They are set out alphabetically with space for you to note ways in which they relate to the needs in your school.

Assessment

'There are no plans to introduce statutory teacher assessment in Key Stages 1 and 2' in geography for the period 1998 and beyond (SCAA, 1997c). However,

> *teachers are required to:*
> *teach geography on the basis of the 1995 Order;*
> *report progress in the subject each year.*
> *Teachers will use their professional judgement to determine the most effective methods of gathering evidence of pupils' progress and the most appropriate way of reporting to parents.*
> (SCAA, 1997c)

It is interesting to note that this SCAA document connects assessment directly to the reporting process rather than informing the teacher's planning and diagnosis of pupils' learning. As a coordinator you need to be able to advise and guide teachers into assessments which are relevant to geography and which will improve the quality of teaching and learning. There are no tests or publication of league tables in the subject and as a result it can become a low priority in teachers' minds. Their concerns lie with SATs in the core subjects. Anything you suggest or offer needs to be realistic and practical. However, you also need to ensure that it fulfils external criteria of 'the extent to which: there are effective systems for assessing pupils' attainment; assessment information is used to inform curriculum planning' (OFSTED, 1995b). The central message here is that within your planning documents you will need to have evidence of how assessment is used within an informed and developing planning process. This can be achieved in a number of ways and these examples are given to help you re-examine your current documents, policies and practice:

- Do teacher's geography lesson plans make reference to what, how and why they will assess in any given lesson?

- Does the geography assesment policy match that of the whole school?

- What range of assessment techniques and evidence do your teachers actually use in geography?

- Are they aware of strategies for building assessment opportunities into learning activities? For instance, do they build geographical vocabulary into new tasks to assess the extent to which children understand and apply it?

- What use do teachers really make of the previous years' reports to parents when preparing their schemes of work and short term plans?

It might also be worth considering the range of evidence teachers use to assess pupils. Geography provides the opportunity to use many sources:

watching pupils at work; their answers to specific questions; field sketches, written work, their ability to use a compass in the field etc.

Teachers can also devise many geographical activities into which assessment can be built: giving directions to other children; accessing a CD-ROM map package; drawing a map.

It will be useful for you to know the process by which information is sent to the secondary school on the transfer of your pupils. If possible, arrange to meet the head of geography. Such meetings may smooth the experiences children have in primary and secondary geography. Some secondary schools have worked with their group of feeder primary schools on examining curriculum continuity in geography. The effectiveness of such work has varied owing to the wide range of localities and experiences from which the primary children come. Discuss the possibility of such discussions with your head: hopefully any developments will make your End of Key Stage 2 assessments of geographical understanding of some use to secondary teachers in addition to the value of reporting to parents.

Foley and Janikoun (1996) suggest a wide range of activities and sources which teachers can use. You may wish to focus on these during your INSET work with staff, if you decide that such work is needed in your school, or with certain staff in order to establish assessment within the planning process.

Differentiation

 One of the most difficult aspects of teaching is to set pupils tasks which are appropriate to their abilities — tasks which challenge them at whatever level of ability and which result in a positive development of skills, understanding and knowledge.　　　　　　　　　　　　　　　(Smith, 1997)

One of your tasks as geography coordinator is to help colleagues design and teach lessons which include differentiated activities. The ultimate, but impossible task in the current climate is for teachers to plan different work for each child. Your task is to assess the extent to which degrees of differentiation are possible within the realities and needs of your school.

A lesson using effective differentiated learning experiences needs a range of resources. The time involved in preparing these can restrict the use teachers make of them. If you feel that much needs to be done throughout the school but that your own time is limited, try to focus on one unit of geography work. Working alongside the teachers currently teaching that unit devise a range of differentiated activities and resources that they could use. Try to create an atmosphere where they feel this is rather special and in which they are really involved. If it is successful you may have established a small team of disciples who will talk enthusiastically about their methods. Your role as coordinator is then to monitor how effective this staff development work actually is in the classroom. Again, it will be a fine balance between how much you do for them to get them started and how far you expect them to be independent.

Another strategy might be to talk about differentiation with other curriculum coordinators. Do they also feel that their own subjects would benefit from some INSET activities? You might then approach the headteacher to see if a staff meeting or event could focus on differentiation. This might be a more effective use of time within your school and raise the level of teachers' discussion across a range of subjects.

If you are attempting to understand how differentiation is planned into geography across the school, it may be worth thinking about a range of processes teachers could use.

Well targeted differentiation needs to be based on teachers knowing what the pupils have already learned. They then need to devise more detailed plans which relate to the Programmes of Study. You can take on an effective role here by becoming involved in the preparation of schemes of work which actually include ideas for a range of differentiated activities.

Teachers need an understanding of how various teaching methods can be used in geography lessons. By observing geography teaching around the school you may be able to establish which of the following are used by teachers:

Differentiation by task
A class could be divided into four ability groups and each one has its own task to complete.

Differentiation by outcome or result
Using whole class teaching, one task is set and different results are expected from each child.

Differentiation by a carefully scaffolded sequence of activities
After a whole class introduction, children begin to work on a set of related tasks. The most able will probably complete all of them.

Differentiation by recording
This can be a useful strategy in geography because the various recording methods can focus on particular geographical skills. For instance, give pupils a set of photogaphs of the school grounds and their tasks are to mark where they think the photographer stood. For some, this will mean placing a sticker on a large scale plan. For others they have to use a compass and also record the direction in which the camera was pointing. Another group might have to record the bearing in which the camera was facing. Other examples in the field might require field sketching, writing a list of words, making a graph of findings or recording data on a data logger.

Geographical enquiries do lend themselves to using differentiated activities. More details and practical ideas on planning for differentiation can be found in *Primary Geographer* 28, January 1997 which is a whole issue devoted to differentiation. Barry Piggott's article in *Primary Geographer* 21, April 1995, pp. 30–32 discusses the details of planning for differentiation in geography.

Environmental education

Pupils have to study aspects of the environment at Key Stages 1 and 2 and have 'first-hand experiences in the local environment which are essential starting points for classroom tasks' (Palmer, 1994). This is an important planning issue because if you study the whole of the National Curriculum at both Key Stages you will find very few other references to environmental education. If it is not planned into the whole curriculum through geography your pupils may have minimal access during their primary school lives. As a geography coordinator you have a key role to play here in managing the extent to which future citizens have the opportunity to develop skills and understanding in this important area.

It could also have implications for your whole school policy. If this policy states that the school aims to develop an understanding of the environment, how human beings interact with it, their effects and responsibilities, then you will need to consider how this is covered in the curriculum. Also, at the time of writing there is a growing interest in the part citizenship education might play in future curriculum developments. This is clearly linked with environmental issues.

Environmental education will be most effective if taught in relation to other areas of the curriculum. Pressure of time will probably demand this anyway in your school. Useful planning ideas and a broad picture of cross-curricular links can be found in *Teaching Environmental Matters through the National Curriculum* (SCAA, 1996a). If you can locate *Curriculum Guidance 7: Environmental Education* (NCC, 1990) it should provide more ideas for cross-curricular work.

If you think you need support try to identify members of staff who might help by becoming involved in planning. The science coordinator could be a useful ally. Real environmental issues in your locality and further afield are essential starting points, but you do need good contacts. A list of these is provided in the resources chapter towards the end of this book.

European dimension

The thematic studies section of the Key Stage 2 Order states that when studying rivers, weather, settlement and environmental change 'contexts should include the United Kingdom and the European Union' (DfE, 1995). One part of your role will be to look at your school context and lead discussion with colleagues about how a European dimension may be developed. Cross-curriculur issues also need to be considered. For instance the art Order requires pupils to be introduced to art genres from 'a variety of cultures, Western and non-Western' (DfE, 1995) as well as your school locality. Some schools have found this to be an interesting way of studying the cultures, landscapes and peoples of other European countries using techniques from art and geography.

The scale and depth to which you coordinate and plan a European dimension into your work will vary. A simple and effective way into this field might be to study a European river using a commercially produced pack. This could be compared with a river in your locality. At the other end of the planning spectrum you may be able to create links with schools abroad and use this source of information as the basis of your work. Recent research (Halocha, 1997b) suggests that these links not only provide a rich learning experience for pupils but can have positive effects on the professional development of teachers.

A wide range of help is available for schools to get such initiatives planned and started. The Central Bureau for Educational Visits and Exchanges is one starting point: details of their facilities are included in the resources chapter of this book. Issues 19 and 29 of *Primary Geographer* provide many examples of how schools are developing an active European dimension as well as details about the numerous resources now available.

Equal opportunities

One of your jobs as coordinator will be to ensure that equal opportunities for all pupils are offered within the planned geography curriculum. As you monitor the written plans and what occurs in practice, use these questions to assess the extent to which equal opportunities really do exist:

■ Is there support from the school management to ensure equal opportunities? For instance, are ways found to financially support some pupils to attend field visits?

■ Do the aims and objectives, curriculum and organisation of the school really promote equal opportunities? Are links with the wider world really built into school aims? You may need to consider the actual amount of time allocated to geography in each year group, for example.

■ Have you established practical ways of monitoring pupil's progress in geography with due regard to gender, attainment, background and ethnicity to ensure that they are treated fairly? For instance, are some geography resources relevant to particular ethnic groups within your school?

■ Are relevant role models encouraged within the teaching of geography. You might consider whether it is always male or female staff who lead field study visits. What role do parents play?

■ Do the geography plans take into account pupils with special educational needs? Do you discuss their needs with the SENCO and where necessary, build geographical work into IEPs?

■ If you have pupils in your school for whom English is an additional language, do you have some suitable geographical resources available for them?

■ Is information technology really planned into the geography curriculum to ensure that pupils have the opportunity 'to develop and apply their information technology (IT) capability in their study of geography' (GA/NCET, 1995).

You may need to look at particular parts of the geography curriculum to ensure equal opportunities are being considered. For instance, do you take into account special educational needs when planning fieldwork activities? How do teachers manage resources in their classrooms to ensure all pupils can make appropriate use of them? Finally, a large amount of legislation exists in the field of equal opportunities. If you are unsure about anything, do ask the headteacher for their advice and access to the relevant documents.

Fieldwork

You will be involved in deciding where fieldwork activities should be planned into the whole curriculum. It is worth asking other coordinators what fieldwork they plan for as it may be possible to combine activities into meaningful studies. Fieldwork takes time and can be expensive, therefore you need to have clear ideas about why it takes place. This helps your justification to both colleagues and parents. A number of planning questions arise, use these to examine your current fieldwork and consider what changes might need to be made. Some will be easy to achieve while others might need major adaptations to the school year.

- When does fieldwork take place?
- How does the current pattern really reinforce progress and continuity in children's learning?
- Do young children only work near the school while the oldest attend the residential visit?
- Where do you go and why are these places chosen?
- Are fieldwork locations part of your own locality, a locality in the UK and even abroad? This is a useful place to point out that contexts in the European Union are encouraged in relation to the thematic studies at Key Stage 2.
- Where do visits take place within particular units of work? Are these ideal? For instance, is a visit most effective at the start, middle or end of a period of study?
- What preparation and follow-up work do children do and how well planned is this?
- Is there scope to replace some visits with new ones which are more appropriate?
- Is it possible (and indeed is there a culture within the staff) for visits to be made at short notice, for instance by walking to the local bridge to watch the river in flood.

These issues are raised because you may find yourself in a school where the visit programme is carved in stone but which may not be an effective means of learning geography. Once again your inter-personal skills and ability to prioritise will become very important. Well planned, well managed and safely carried out activities can have a really lasting and positive effect on children so your effort to establish a quality programme should provide many rewards.

If you need support in developing and planning a fieldwork programme a number of sources are available to help you:

- the *Fieldwork in Action* series of books (May et al. 1993–1996) published by the Geographical Association;
- LEA advisory teachers and subject inspectors;
- LEA field study centre wardens (these may be in your county or further afield);
- private residential centres and activity groups. (It is important that these adhere to legal requirements discussed in the fieldwork chapter).

Flexibility

Much of this book discusses the need for effective planning and coordination. You will have many pressures on you to ensure this happens. But because geography is about a world that is constantly changing, part of your role is to encourage teachers to build these changes and events into their daily work.

> Perhaps the teacher can spend a few minutes before lunch using a globe to see where the smog caused by forest fires is affecting the Far East (a news item as this is being written).
>
> The new litter bins have arrived for the playground. Could some children work with the school caretaker at breaktime to decide where they should be located so pupils will really use them?

Brief activities like these can help develop geographical skills, knowledge and understanding. Such events could never be planned in the official planning documents. Keep alert as to what is happening in school, the locality and the wider world and you will be able to support teachers in bringing this degree of flexibility into their everyday teaching.

Information Technology

The author's work takes him into many schools around the country. A consistent pattern seen in school planning at all levels is the small extent to which information technology is carefully planned into whole school plans, schemes of work and individual lesson plans. While the development of this situation is clearly the main responsibility of the IT coordinator in your school, you can play an effective part in moving this process forward.

The pace of technological development is fast but teachers' knowledge and confidence in using IT in the classroom is failing to keep up with these changes. The IT coordinator has a big job to do. This can be helped if other colleagues can feed in ideas and support in the same way as you will be helped in your work. Study the geography whole school planning to see where/if IT has been included. Do you have evidence for this actually taking place in the classroom? If it is not try to discuss with colleagues how you might support them in developing this. Remember that the IT coordinator will be looking for a friend who has practical ideas about applying IT across the curriculum. Working together can help to reduce your workload as coordinators.

Up to date and practical ideas on planning information technology into the primary geography curriculum can be found in Martin (1995), Chambers and Donert (1996) and *Primary Geography: a pupil's entitlement to IT* (GA/NCET, 1995).

Localities

These need careful consideration when planning at all levels. Re-read the locality requirements for Key Stages 1 and 2 on pages 87 and 89 of *Key Stages 1 and 2 of the National Curriculum* (DfE, 1995).

> Two localities need to be studied at Key Stage 1 and three at Key Stage 2. You have a number of planning questions to keep in mind when looking at your whole school geography plans.
>
> Where will these be located?
>
> Will major blocks of time be allocated or will smaller periods be used allowing the children to regularly re-visit locality work within, for example, river studies?

GA/NCET (1995) suggest the following planning stages to effect pupils' entitlement to IT:

Evaluate the opportunities you provide for using IT in geography;
how IT enhances geography teaching;
the extent to which IT is planned into geography.

Plan the development of IT into your geography development plan;
to develop a scheme of work for geography which has clear references to IT.
to do this over a realistic time span (1 or 2 years).

Action carry out the development plan;
implement the scheme of work.

Monitor and review

Do the pupils have opportunities to use IT to:

- support investigations and enquiry?
- access different sources of information?
- recognise patterns and relationships?
- evaluate its effects on everyday life?

Are pupils able to:
- ask and answer geographical questions?
- identify, collect and classify relevant information?
- analyse patterns and relationships?
- talk about the impact of IT?

What do pupils know and understand? Has IT contributed to this?

(GA/NCET, 1995)

You may then take this information back to the evaluation part of the cycle as you continue to develop your planning role.

To what extent will the chosen localities be the focus for developing work in geographical skills and thematic studies? If this can be achieved pupils will learn within a more meaningful environment and be able to apply their understanding more easily.

Could your locality and the contrasting UK locality be studied side by side for at least some of the time? Useful comparisons can be made and links such as those with other schools can provide interesting sources of data.

Are activities planned which will allow pupils to understand how localities are linked with the wider world around them? A danger of thinking in terms of localities is that they are studied as isolated parts of the world.

What relevant links may be planned with other subjects? One example is whether children will understand your locality better if the geographical aspects of the school locality are studied alongside the local history study unit in the history Orders.

To what extent will you plan locality study as part of a spiral curriculum in which pupils will work on their own locality at a number of times during life in primary school?

Although you are not required to study a European locality, the Orders clearly suggest that the thematic studies in Key Stage 2 may be developed within European contexts. Some schools have found this to be an excellent way of planning a European dimension into their curriculum, sometimes linking it with their policy on the teaching of modern foreign languages. Equally, at Key Stage 1 a thematic study may be carried out on 'the quality of the environment in any locality, either in the United Kingdom or overseas' (DfE, 1995). Some schools use the flexibility within this wording to develop fascinating work on a European location, introducing children to the wider world at an early age. This is in contrast to other schools where a planning model based on the notion of studying places further afield only occurs as the children get older. This may be an planning issue that you wish to raise in your school.

Multiculturalism

There are a number of ways of examining your planning in relation to multiculturalism.

One is to consider the extent to which you really do plan to build in the experiences of any pupils and adults in your school who come from various cultural backgrounds. This approach also includes considering how much you draw on the community around the school and plan it into your geography curriculum. By starting with pupils' real life experiences, you will help to make aspects of your geographical work more meaningful to them. It is also a way of celebrating and recognising the value of their experiences and ways of life. Careful planning is needed to ensure that your colleagues are aware of the need to look at similarities as well as the interesting differences between groups of people around the world. Using such an approach can also mean that you gain access to a wide range of relevant resources and contacts to use in your geography lessons.

The requirement to study a range of contrasting localities gives some excellent opportunities for the development of a multicultural dimension in your school curriculum. It may be approached through the study of foods, customs, languages, homes, costumes, stories and history from around the world. While these studies should be based in localities, they can be an opportunity to show children how such places are linked with the wider world. Effective planning and carefully chosen resources will help children begin to understand issues from various points of view. They may begin to understand that a eurocentric view of the world may need to be questioned. North-south questions will arise and perhaps even the notion of what really is a developed country? Using techniques of geographical enquiring, pupils may begin to collect and analyse evidence which will help them start to understand the variety of cultural similarities and differences around the world.

There may well be close links with the RE curriculum in your school. It might be worthwhile discussing these with the RE coordinator to see if some aspects of your curriculum planning work may be done together. This could strengthen progress and continuity within your whole school plans. You may wish to involve organisations such as Worldaware or Oxfam in your studies. Help and advice may be available from a Development Education Centre if you have one near your school. An LEA adviser may have responsibility for multiculturalism and be pleased to discuss ways of planning it effectively into your geography curriculum.

Progression and continuity

A geography coordinator has a number of tasks to achieve in relation to progression and continuity in children's learning and understanding:

- being actively involved in all aspects of geography planning;
- supporting teachers in their own understanding of what progression means in geography;
- monitoring teaching and learning for effective use of progression.

Chambers and Donert (1996) suggest that 'progression is the careful and deliberate sequencing of learning so that children can build their current learning on previous experience and also prepare for future learning'. This has a number of important implications for the geography coordinator to consider.

Geographical units of work are often located in blocks of time within the whole school plan. Some work may be of a more continuous nature. If the majority of pupils' geographical experiences are in blocked units of time you need to consider the extent to which these are effective in ensuring progression. Are pupils really able to take their learning from one unit, retain previous understanding and apply it to new activities? Or does the time gap make this hard? Subjects such as mathematics provide pupils with daily experiences and consequently children become used to thinking mathematically. The suggested time allowance for geography at Key Stages 1 and 2 would mean that this system would only give a few minutes per day! However, if blocked units of geography are the chosen planning format you may be able to help staff identify opportunities for reinforcing geographical skills and understanding even when geography is not the main focus of attention. How can this work in practice?

Resources

At Key Stage I you may distribute a range of inflatable globes around the infant department. If you can also provide some teacher resources such as *Placing Places* (Catling, 1996a) they will find practical ideas for using globes in the classroom.

You might support Key Stage 2 teachers by locating some web sites covering a recent volcanic eruption and fixing a guide chart to their computer which will allow pupils to access easily new sources of geographical information.

These strategies are useful ways of leading staff to look for effective ways of ensuring that geographical experiences progress throughout the school days and years. Your role is to find that balance between spoon-feeding them and just providing enough support to give them the confidence to eventually take the initiative.

At Key Stage 1 teachers can be encouraged to use and extend children's geographical vocabulary. For instance, when explaining where objects are in the classroom, they can deliberately use words such as left, right, beyond and if compass point words are on the walls then north, south, east and west can be added to these instructions.

At Key Stage 2 teachers can take a few minutes at various points in the week to talk about world and national events in the news. If, for example, a globe and a map of Europe are readily available in classrooms they will find it easier to do this. You can help facilitate such progression in geography by trying to provide useful resources and offering ideas to teachers.

These activities may well not appear in teachers' planning documents. It is more a question of colleagues being aware of a range of strategies which can reinforce and link the major geographical activities within the planned curriculum. Reference to these methods may appear in your geography policy. For instance, if you refer back to the policy for Newtown Infant School, you will see that each classroom is resourced with geographical materials so that teachers have some things readily at hand to make the most of opportunities as they arise during the course of the school day. You can help by arranging for these resources to be available.

The geography units of work should provide many opportunities for children to learn and extend their use of geographical skills. You can play an important role in working with teachers to ensure that the experiences they have will grow and extend. Look across the whole school curriculum for signs of progress and continuity. For instance, in the mathematics scheme pupils will be learning to use grid references and coordinates. Where do these experiences occur and do they link in with where they are planned in the geography units of work? You may find that higher expectations are made in mathematics lessons and that progression and continuity between geography and maths needs some re-examination. Are pupils actually aware that skills they are learning in mathematics can be applied to geographical activities and enquiries?

With the growing emphasis being placed on mathematics and English in the primary curriculum the application of these skills in the real world may need some monitoring. Are we teaching children to jump through a number of learning hoops in order to achieve good SAT results or will they leave school with some awareness of how their learning can be used in the future?

Progression in fieldwork will also need to be considered. Teachers will be planning to use a number of locations for fieldwork. Various aspects of skills, places and themes will, hopefully, be planned into these experiences. But will they allow pupils to make progress in developing their geographical understanding? It can be a daunting job to analyse just what is happening on fieldwork, even if the aims are well documented in teachers' planning. Bland et al. (1996) suggest that by looking at fieldwork from five points of view you may be able to assess the quality of progress and continuity that exists.

1   Skills and techniques.
2   The difficulty of task and level of supervision.
3   Places and themes.
4   Geographical ideas and concepts.
5   Issues and problems under investigation.

Take one at a time and study the various levels of planning to see if the structure of your fieldwork experiences do contain progress and continuity. You might also be looking to see what the balance is between the parts. If you find that there is a heavy emphasis on skills, you may need to consider how this could be adapted and what aspects require greater emphasis.

Another useful structure for assessing progress and continuity is offered by May and Cook (1993). When you are studying plans and observing activities they suggest that useful information about the quality of geographical enquiry can be found by focusing on the following areas.

1   Increasing independence   — in planning
                                                    — in preparation
                                                    — in execution
                                                    — in evaluation

2 Increasing depth of study
3 Increasing sophistication of technique in — data gathering
                                           — data handling
                                           — interpretation
                                           — presentation
4 Increasing rigour throughout

One example from the third suggestion illustrates what you may see:

During enquiries into local weather patterns . . .

Year 1 pupils collect outside temperatures using a simple thermometer in one place. They present their results in a small bar graph to show a week's readings.

Year 4 pupils investigate a range of sites chosen by the teacher around the school to see what variations in microclimates exist. They present their findings together and include some written ideas about why the differences occur.

Year 6 pupils collect data over half a term from around the school using sites they have to justify. They feed the data into a computer program allowing them to analyse it in more depth and present it in various ways. They compare their findings with data sent by pupils at a school in their contrasting locality. They offer explanations for their findings.

Special needs

'Geography is about relationships between people and places. The subject itself is more accessible to pupils with learning difficulties than some other National Curriculum subjects' (Sebba, 1995). There are a number of planning issues relating to pupils' access to the geography curriculum which you need to consider.

Geography is a very practical subject and will probably involve a variety of fieldwork experiences. An effective coordinator will be able to offer advice to teachers about ways in which pupils with special needs may have access to meaningful geographical experiences. The following case studies are given to suggest ideas about what this means in practice. Hopefully, they will start you thinking about issues and needs which are specific to your school and some ways in which they might sensitively be addressed.

Case study 1

A school had a number of pupils with visual impairment working within a mainstream situation. Teachers planned for the use of a wide variety of maps, plans and aerial photographs. These pupils had difficulty using the resources, especially the aerial photographs. A Year 4 teacher asked if a group of her pupils with normal vision could make some 'touch' aerial photographs for the special needs pupils to work from. They had to identify the features they wished to show. Materials were carefully selected. They chose corrugated card for ploughed fields, felt for pasture land, sand paper for beaches and foil paper for water. They then worked alongside the visually impaired children as these resources were used. This involved extensive use of geographical vocabulary and the teacher also found it to be a useful assessment activity.

Case study 2

A school with a strong fieldwork policy wanted pupils to have equal access to a residential visit. One Year 5 pupil was wheelchair bound. The Year 6 residential visit to Wales could have posed a problem. The geography coordinator knew that the boy would be going on the visit in a year's time. Therefore, when she made her visit the previous year, she discussed their needs with the centre manager. They examined the routes and locations they would be using. Additional volunteer help in the locality was arranged. With careful forward planning that pupil was able to experience all parts of the visit.

Your special needs coordinator should be able to offer specific advice on planning for individual children in your school. Indeed, you may become involved in developing IEPs to ensure geography is included within them. Sebba (1991) provides special needs planning ideas and SCAA (1996b) gives examples of good practice in planning for pupils with profound and multiple learning difficulties.

Units of work

These are the building blocks for your geography curriculum. They will have developed over time in your school and the current whole school plan represents a long history of decision making. You may have seen them evolve or you may be a new member of staff. As the geography coordinator you will need to study the range of units to see if they really are effective vehicles for developing geographical activities and understanding.

Geography work in some schools is restricted because little thought has been given to what the focus and content of various units can actually offer to the subjects which are intended to be taught within them. If you do think some need adapting or changing, it cannot be done overnight. There may be knock-on effects across the curriculum and indeed this is often cited by other staff as a good reason for leaving things as they are. As a starting point, identify one unit which stands out as needing attention and work on that. If you are successful and teachers see that the new title, focus and content are an improvement, you have more chance of making other changes at a later date.

Take a look at how long each unit of work is. Many schools provide blank year planning grids broken up into half term slots. While this may be an easy way of breaking up the planning process it can often lead to too much or too little time being spent on particular units. Do you really need to spend a whole half term on the distant locality? Might it be better to split this into three and four week blocks of work for a year group? This method helps to spread geographical experiences across the school year. With recommended times of 36 hours for geography over Key Stages 1 and 45 throughout Key Stage 2, you have to ensure that time is used effectively.

A final planning point to consider is whether to make your units of work place or theme based. A unit of work based on a place might focus on a contrasting locality in India. Within this you could plan aspects on the river, weather, settlements and environmental issues if the locality offers suitable content. A unit of work based on the theme 'Rivers' might focus on a European river and include some fieldwork at your local river. There are advantages and disadvantages in both methods.

A unit focused on place can become overloaded, but a strong advantage of this method is that geographical enquiries are centred around a real place which can be seen in a wider context. The benefit of basing units of work on themes is that they can be easier to manage for some non-specialist teachers. It also makes planning the locality requirements more straightforward.

A big disadvantage of planning theme-based units of work called, for example, 'Rivers' is that important relationships within the real world can be lost. If you then study 'Settlements' at another time, the connections between them may not be apparent to the pupils. However, if you select a place in which to study rivers and settlements, it becomes much easier to plan activities which help to explain relationships in the real world.

There has been a tendency for schools to take the headings given in the Orders and design units of work around them. Part of your role might be to re-examine this so that new units are created which help children to understand the real world more effectively.

Part four Monitoring for quality

Chapter 11
Assessment, recording and reporting

Chapter 12
The geography coordinator and OFSTED inspections

Assessment, recording and reporting

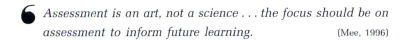

Assessment is an art, not a science ... the focus should be on assessment to inform future learning. (Mee, 1996)

When considering assessment, recording and reporting a geography coordinator should look at various factors:

- you have a responsibility to monitor what geography is being taught, how it is being taught and the outcomes of that teaching on pupils' learning;

- you need to understand how teachers use the assessment, recording and reporting cycle to inform their planning;

- you need to be aware of the assessment evidence needed by different people and how they might use it;

- you need to collect evidence to inform your judgments and support the need for any changes;

- you have to develop skills in creating two types of broad perspective on what is happening in your school. The first is the ability to monitor children's geographical learning as they move up through the school. The second is the ability to see how the whole school geography policy is changing over time and affecting overall standards of learning.

These are demanding activities and rather different from the assessment perspectives of a class teacher. This chapter will discuss the things you have to do as geography coordinator and some of the issues which arise. A useful way to begin may be to discuss the assessment of children just as they start at school.

Baseline assessment

Unless you work in a junior or middle school, you are likely to be involved in baseline assessment. From September 1998 all children will be assessed when they begin school. Schools will be able to choose whether or not to use assessment schemes that include 'knowledge and understanding of the world' which is one of the headings created under the initiative. At some point schools will have to decide whether they wish to include this area and this is an issue you will need to discuss with all colleagues. If the staff decide that it would be useful to have some evidence of the incoming children's knowledge and understanding of the world, you should press for the use of a scheme which includes this. This point has been emphasised because it seems that even with such young pupils there are opportunities within the legal framework for schools to marginalise the role of geography.

A leaflet has been published for parents which explains baseline assessment. It includes a section called 'how can I help my child do well at school?' This has no direct reference to helping them develop any basic geographical or spatial skills, which is an issue you may like to discuss with the head and member of staff responsible for your pupil entry programme. They may appreciate your advice on things parents can do to assist their children. *Looking at Children's Learning* (SCAA, 1997f) provides information on how the initiative will work.

The whole area is an important issue for schools as it relates to monitoring their performance and the value-added nature of their work. If geography is left out at this early stage, what chance does it have later on?

Assessment

Geography curriculum coordinators need to be aware of the legal requirements for assessment in their subject:

- There is no requirement to conduct End-of-Key Stage Assessments in geography in 1997. This means there is no obligation for teachers to record and report children's attainments in the form of levels for the subject at the end of the key stage.

- Teachers are required to:
  — teach geography on the basis of the 1995 Order;
  — report progress in the subject each year.

- Teachers will use their professional judgment to determine the most effective method of gathering evidence of pupils' progress and the most appropriate way of reporting to parents.

- There are no plans to introduce statutory teacher assessment in Key Stages 1 and 2.   (SCAA, 1997c)

It appears that this is the context in which you will be working for the forseeable future. Your role will be to assist teachers in developing and using assessment methods which:
- can help us to understand more fully pupils' progress in their learning;
- can guide the response in our teaching to what we learn about pupils;
- can help us raise pupil achievement.

(Butt, Lambert and Telfer, 1995)

Colleagues will have considerable expertise in assessment. Some will be in the form of skills in informative assessment while other parts will come from experience of administering SATs. If possible try to capitalise on the fact that assessment in geography is not connected to the professional and public pressures of school performance and league tables. It really is there to help them understand pupils' learning in geography and how they can develop it further. For this reason, you

Teachers may need guidance about what patterns and processes mean in geography. Patterns are the ways in which human and physical features are set out in the environment. Pupils may find a pattern in traffic flows outside their school. They may observe the way in which village and towns grow up on river crossing points. Processes refers to the ways things change in the landscape. A river moves stones and pebbles and gradually wears a new course in the landscape. The building of a new supermarket affects the way shoppers use the local shopping parade.

should try to ensure that all aspects of assessment, recording and reporting in geography are 'simple, straightforward and manageable' (SCAA, 1997a).

There are a number of professional aims for assessing children's geographical work:

- to help teachers plan future learning experiences;
- to enable reports to parents to be accurate and fair;
- to allow pupils to understand how well they are achieving in geography;
- to enable the coordinator to assess how the subject is progressing throughout the whole school;
- to provide evidence for external inspection of the school's quality of provision.

The coordinator's role is to develop and monitor practical ways of achieving these aims. In order to do this we have to establish ways

 in which children's progress can be identified and assessed. Children can make progress in:

- *knowledge and understanding of places;*
- *knowledge and understanding of patterns and processes;*
- *knowledge and understanding of environmental relationships and issues;*
- *ability to undertake enquiry and to use skills.*

(SCAA, 1997a)

Teachers may need support in developing their skills in assessing progress in geography. What type of evidence can they use? What are they looking for? How might progression be identified in the subject? If you need ideas for helping colleagues SCAA have produced a booklet for geography coordinators and teachers entitled *Expectations in Geography at Key Stages 1 and 2* (SCAA, 1997b). It uses samples of children's work in geography. It may give you some ideas for developing staff skills and understanding. You could use the examples from the book or even better your children's work. Adapt the ideas and find examples which reflect the work going on in your school. For instance, if you exchange e-mail letters with another European school, what can they tell you about children's geographical understanding?

Another part of your role will be helping colleagues identify opportunities and evidence for making assessments in geography. They will be able to make formative assessments from a range of sources:

    written work
    spoken activities
    maps, plans and sketches
    group activities
    fieldwork
    audio and video recordings
    information technology materials, e.g. e-mails, desk top publishing
    models
    photographs
    comments from other people, e.g. helpers on fieldwork

You can probably think of other sources avaliable in your school. It is impossible to use and keep everything so discussions with colleagues may identify what evidence will be used and kept for a particular unit of work. This is an important point for you in helping to decide the range of materials needed for inclusion in your subject portfolio. It can be useful to ask staff to let you have a small sample of work from the range of ability levels within their class. Some coordinators have also found it useful to track a small number of pupils right through the school. As they complete each unit their teachers provide evidence of geographical achievement. This could represent their developing understanding of geographical processes, e.g. how a river works or their ability to represent the world through map-making.

Evidence of activities and teaching methods can also be useful. Videos of class assemblies, photographs of children working at the river and computer discs of pupils' work are all examples of assessment evidence you build into your portfolio to assess the overall development of geography throughout the school.

Recording

The methods used for recording geography will need to relate to the agreed record-keeping policies in your school.

'For most primary school teachers, geography comes fairly well down the list of assessment priorities' (Wiegand, 1997). The record keeping system will therefore need to be simple, easy to use and of practical value to the teachers. You will also need to be aware of the dangers inherent in various recording methods. If you develop a tick list approach, will you simply be encouraging teachers to record a 'has done' set of information rather than 'understands and can apply'? For example, it would be fairly simple to create a tick list for the teaching of mapwork skills. Children could be trained to jump through a number of mapwork hoops. The real test would be whether they can apply them to the real world and in solving geographical problems. Fortunately, we are moving away from a tick list era of assessment. However, if you are taking over responsibility for an existing geography assessment policy it may be worth looking at the paperwork and assessment guidelines to see what hidden or transparent messages are given to teachers. If you find that simple tick lists for geography skills still exist, this may be an area in which you decide to take some early action. Butt, Lambert and Telfer (1995) recommend keeping the following points in mind when deciding what to record and how to record it:

■ record significant progress;
■ record your assessments, rather than coverage of the subject; your curriculum planning will do the latter;
■ aim for quality of assessment, rather than quantity;
■ records should be consistent;
■ records should be fit for the purpose you intend.

If you are beginning a discussion with staff about record keeping in geography this list may provide a useful starting point for a short staff development discussion and workshop.

A further job for the coordinator is to help staff develop their skills in keeping useful records within a subject. Your starting point is that geography will be low on people's priority but you are also responsible for ensuring that parents receive an accurate report of their child's progress in the subject. One way into this is to work with colleagues on developing record keeping within a unit of work and then building out from this. The following example illustrates how this might work.

A teacher in a village school is about to begin a study of their contrasting UK locality with Year 5 children. It is an urban, industrial area. They have a link with a school in their locality which she has carefully planned with those teachers. She wants to both establish her pupils' understanding of other places and begin to get them to develop some lines of enquiry. She starts the work by asking the class what they know about cities. How did they get this information? Have they been to a city? Have they seen them on television? Do they visit relations living in a town or city? She then asks them to draw what they think it might be like and encourages them to add geographical words around their drawing. The next stage is to ask each child to write down a question they have about the locality. These might include

Are there any farms in the city?
What job has your mum got?
Does everybody live in a flat?
How many children are there in your school?
Where do you go to play?
Have you got any shops because the one in our village closed down last year?
Are you scared to go outside at night in such a big place?

They will collate these questions and send them to a class in the contact school. These activities give her a broad picture of where the children are starting from. The drawings may suggest that her pupils see cities as noisy, dangerous places. If they use a limited range of geographical vocabulary this can provide starting points to devise activities which will extend this and help pupils to describe and explain the world. The activities are non-threatening for the children and are meaningful as they are part of their contact with another group of children. Assessment is also built into these geographical activities and she uses it to inform the planning of this unit of work.

At the end of the unit of work each child prepares a brief guidebook for a newcomer to the city locality they have been studying. This provides opportunities to use geographical skills such as drawing maps with keys, explaining what the land is used for and what it is like to live there. This record of their understanding can be used to help assess the extent to which they have an understanding of that part of the city. She may also refer back to the evidence collected at the start of the unit of study. In addition, she will have been making 'informed diagnostic assessment' (Wiegand, 1997) throughout this work to guide and focus particular activities. The pupils' work can also be used at parents' evenings as a basis for discussing their progress and achievement in some aspects of geography.

This example illustrates how assessment activities can be built into everyday work. Pupils probably do not view them as forms of assessment and teachers should not see them as a burden. 'If record systems do not provide a significant contribution to teaching and learning there is little point in maintaining them' (Dearing Report, 1993).

Reporting

You will probably be able to identify three main forms of reporting pupils' progress in geography in your school:
- annual written reports to parents
- verbal reports/discussions at meetings with parents

- written evidence provided for the secondary school to which your pupils transfer.

What can you do as a coordinator to enhance and monitor the quality of these reporting processes?

Annual written reports to parents

It may be worthwhile discussing with the head the possibility of having the opportunity to read a representative sample, if not all, of the reports going out to parents. This may give you a picture of what the staff perceive to be needed in reporting progress in geography. It may highlight a particular member of staff who can crisply and clearly explain to parents what progress in primary geography is all about. It might identify another who relies on the level descriptions for all the words she uses in her report and you may judge that there is some uncertainty about how to report effectively. Incidentally, not all staff may realise that level descriptions are non-statutory in geography and may or may not be used in any stage of the assessment process.

By reading the reports carefully you may also be able to pick up trends in teaching style and content around the school. Some teachers may give a particular emphasis to some aspects of geography. For instance, one teacher may only make reference to geographical skills in every report he writes. With additional evidence you may be able to build a clearer picture of the geography teaching taking place in that class.

Verbal reports/ discussions at meetings with parents

These will be much harder to monitor as you will probably be meeting your parents at the same time. If you think it is important to develop the profile of geography in your school, you may wish to develop this through parents' evenings. The suggestion box shows the two main ways of raising the profile of geography in the school through a parents' evening.

Using parents' evenings to develop the profile of geography

Encourage and remind staff to raise particular geographical activities and events which have taken place. Perhaps a class had a really successful day visit to the local river. Could the teacher make a point of using assessment evidence from the visit when discussing pupils' progress? Can links be made to other subjects such as mathematics and English? Offer to discuss with colleagues the things they might wish to highlight during a parents' evening. For instance, a Key Stage 2 child may still need many experiences to develop spatial skills and vocabulary. The parents might appreciate practical ideas on how they can help to develop these at home.

Parents are able to look around the school and classrooms during parents' evenings. Could you arrange to have a video playing in the entrance hall which shows the recent residential visit? Perhaps pupils wrote and recorded the commentary as a planned part of the writing and speaking sections of the English Orders? The content, accuracy, clarity and enthusiasm of such a presentation can say much about children's progress in both geography and English. Geography displays and samples of work can also be set out. This not only reports to the parents of those pupils taking part in the activity but can give positive messages to everyone who sees them.

Written evidence provided for the secondary school

This will be closely tied to the whole school policy on transfer procedures. Perhaps one of the most useful things you can do in your role as geography coordinator is develop a positive working relationship with geography colleagues in the secondary school. There are a number of reasons for doing this:

- It can provide a mechanism which allows some progress and continuity between the hard work you have helped to coordinate and that which will be developed following transfer. A practical example can illustrate this. If you do some work in the locality which is repeated at the same, or an even simpler level at secondary school, there is every chance of killing children's interest in geography. It will be hard enough to retain this at the secondary level with the pressure of other subjects and the need to make examination choices. If secondary colleagues have clear and simple reports of experiences and attainment it may make continuity and progression more effective.

- A developing understanding of the pressures and demands each other experiences can help teachers at Key Stages 2 and 3 have a clearer idea of the effects their teaching can have on children's overall progress in geography. Knowing that Key Stage 3 geography teachers have to work with pupils from perhaps ten feeder schools is a sobering thought. At best it can also inform decision-making at both Key Stages 2 and 3. This is not a question of one sector dictating to the other what should be taught, but you may move to a situation where that is the case. An experienced headteacher or liaison teacher can help you tread carefully through a potential minefield! They've probably been there before.

- Positive contacts and relationships can take you beyond reporting pupil progress. It may be possible to share resources and even teacher expertise. Can you build geography into the transfer process by working through the liaison teacher to arrange for a secondary colleague to work with Year 6 pupils? Do they have a link to a weather satellite which might provide some useful resources for work in your school? At a broader level, if you really did make links with that Italian headteacher, can some secondary pupils help with the translation of letters and e-mails between the two countries?

A broader view of assessment

So much of what teachers have to do in terms of assessment is now related to testing pupils. As we move into the next millenium more and more testing is taking place: SATs are conducted; results are published and league tables are scrutinised. 'Failing' schools are identified. Evidence is provided mainly from pupils' performance in English, mathematics and science. However, if we consider the view of Gipps (1994) who claims that 'Assessment is not an exact science, and we must stop presenting it as such', subjects such as geography may have an important part to play in assessing and reporting those aspects of children's learning which are so much harder to quantify but are no less important:

> To what extent do they understand the ways in which people affect and change our world?
> Are they aware of the many similarities and some differences between people in other countries?
> Have they begun to make informed opinions on what they feel about various places and issues?
> What do they feel and think when they visit various places?
> Do they really enjoy learning to understand about the world in which they all live?

These and many other questions relate to a broader view of children as human beings who live in particular social and physical environments. Assessment through geography can provide insights into the development in these important aspects of their growth as observing, thinking and feeling people.

The geography coordinator and OFSTED inspections

❛ *One benefit is that it concentrates the mind — rather like facing an execution, some say!* (Harris, 1996)

Hopefully your experience of OFSTED inspections will be less painful and less permanent. One way in which to survive and hopefully benefit from the experience is to break down what you as the geographer coordinator have to do:

> before the inspection
> during the inspection
> after the inspection

The ideas suggested in the following three sections are not in order of importance or priority. They are intended to provide a checklist to support you through each stage of the process. Your understanding of the school's situation and the way in which your role will link with everyone else will affect the order, importance and depth to which each will apply.

Before the inspection

First, take a deep breath. Inspections can be stressful and one way to control this is to work out a list of things you will need to do and a timescale in which to do them. If you are unsure about any aspect of the inspection, ask the headteacher for advice. Use other sources of guidance that may help, for example, your LEA advisory/inspection service will probably provide support in a number of ways. Do not be afraid to seek help from the specialists: the geography inspector/advisory teachers are there to assist you and probably have extensive experience already. They will go through your documents in detail, offer advice, check your resources and put what you do in a wider context. Having to discuss and justify your work will also be a valuable learning experience.

Talk to coordinators in schools that have already been inspected. If you are amazingly lucky they may have had the same team who will be visiting you! This will help to make you familiar both with what happens during an inspection and things that will be relevant to your situation. Learn from the successes and failures of others. Read inspection reports from other schools as this will give you a feel for what might be written about geography. It may make you feel more comfortable or perhaps ring some alarm bells.

Read through the OFSTED Handbook *Guidance on the Inspection of Nursery and Primary Schools* (HMSO, 1995). Note the parts which may be relevant to you. For instance, section 5.5 'Partnership with parents and the community' may be appropriate, especially if you want to emphasise the extent to which you use the locality and people within it. This can be useful during the inspection when perhaps in your interview you clarify the quality of the geography work and how it feeds into the broader life of the school. Good preparation will give you confidence and knowledge to show your work in its best light.

Following this background work, you then need to ask yourself some questions. The following ten ideas are adapted from Richardson (1995).

1 Check your geography policy thoroughly.
Is your policy in a draft, final or rewrite stage? Make this clear.
Refer back to Chapters 9 and 10 to check the presentation, content and structure of the geography policy. Is it up to date? Remember that what it says

should be happening in school. It may be that a major new initiative has been put into practice but this is not in your policy. Accidents do happen, so check everything for consistency.

Do all the staff understand the policy and actually use it? Inspectors may do some cross checking for consistency across the school.

Make sure your job descrpition is accurate.

Check that the geography resources list is up to date.

2   Do the schemes of work cover all the requirements of the Order?
Can progress and continuity be easily mapped through the schemes of work?
Is teachers' short term planning up to date?
Is the work actually interesting, exciting and relevant to children?

3   Are all levels of pupil ability catered for in geography lessons?
Are resources available for effective differentiation?

4   Are assessment, recording and reporting tasks manageable and useful in backing up professional judgments?
Are teacher and school records up to date?

5   Is fieldwork really a part of geographical lessons? If it is planned to take place during the inspection, don't change it. Good fieldwork is essential for geography and inspectors are required to observe it if at all possible. If done well it can be a great asset.

6   Will geographical enquiry really be seen by the inspectors during their visit?
Are children asking questions, handling data and discussing their findings about the real world?
Will pupils really know what they are doing and why they are doing it?

7   Are geography resources and information technology used in lessons?
Will pupils be able to show that they can use skills from previous work?

8   Can the geography resources be found and easily used?
    Are they up to date? If not, some careful weeding may
    be needed.
    Repair useful but worn items. Are other relevant parts of
    the school in good and workable condition? For instance,
    what is the state of the wild area? Does everything in the
    weather station work?

9   Am I up to date on recent developments in primary
    geography? For instance, if a regional Geographical
    Association Conference is planned in your area before
    the inspection, go along, find out the latest thinking and
    get ideas. Be ready to tell the inspector ways in which
    this visit was useful for your role.

10 Are pupils and staff in your school enjoying geography?
    This really can come across during an inspection. If
    you're enthusiastic there's a good chance it will rub off
    on some people if not everyone.

As well as being a checklist for things you may need to do,
they can also be a reminder of what is going well which
should be highlighted to the inspectors. If the inspection is
to take place at a time when a major geography unit will
be taught, spend time with those teachers, giving them
additional support, advice and encouragement. They will
probably appreciate your efforts and if this enhances their
work, a particularly favourable geography paragraph could
appear in your school's report.

Before the inspection you will be asked to produce the
following documentation:

The school geography policy
Schemes of work for all age ranges in your school
A list of geography resources
Your job description

In addition, check that your personal portfolio is up to date
and can be used in discussion with the inspectors. A range
of geographical work from children in all age groups should

be collected. Bring together all the other evidence available to show what has been happening in geography. This could include a video of the last residential visit, photographs of geographical work in school, displays and visitors who came to help in geography lessons. If you have a special long term project such as a link with another school in Europe, get together an exhibition of e-mails, letters, exchanged artefacts and other connected items.

If it fits in with the whole school approach to the inspection, arrange for all these materials to be on clear display for the inspectors to see. Sell the good things you have been doing. This is especially important if the inspection is to take place when no major geographical work is planned. The inspectors need evidence and it is your job to exhibit and explain what you have been doing.

Inspectors may ask other teachers about things which they will cross-check with you. For instance, what practical support do you give them in geography? What resources are available for developing mapping skills and where are they kept? Why have you chosen to use the Isle of Wight for your residential study visit? If you know your colleagues well, you should know where to have some discussions to try to remind people of some key issues. For example, the newly qualified teacher is going on the residential visit with a more experienced colleague, but may not yet have been fully briefed about this or have any previous experience. You can help to ensure that staff are clear about what happens in geography and why.

All these preparations will help to give you confidence and remind you about many points you can have at your fingertips when you are involved in formal and informal interviews.

During the inspection

Inspectors will collect evidence about geography, and indeed everything else, from a number of sources:

the documents you provide for them;
observing lessons;
observations around the school;
studying samples of pupils' work;
talking with children;
discussions with you and other adults in the school.

Where there is sufficient evidence for geography the final report will include an evaluation of

■ pupils' attainment in relation to national expectations or standards, drawing on evidence of what pupils know, understand and can do by the end of the relevant stage;

■ progress made in relation to pupils' prior attainment;

■ pupils' attitude to learning;

■ any strengths and weaknesses in teaching and other factors which contribute to the standards achieved in the subject. (HMSO, 1995)

There is very little you can do to affect these once the inspection is in progress. What really counts is the work you have done before. For instance, inspectors will talk to pupils and seek to establish their interest, attitudes towards and confidence in geography. If, as part of your everyday life in school, you can find time to talk to children about their geographical work, show your interest and enthusiasm, it can have a positive effect on their attitude to learning. This takes time to build up. It's a skill which an effective coordinator can develop as part of good professional practice, regardless of the positive benefits which may emerge during an inspection.

During the inspection find time to talk to any teachers who are doing geographical work. Offer a listening ear and any advice and resources they might need. Feedback any information you are getting from other colleagues which might help them.

Keep an eye on the geography resources to ensure they remain well organised throughout the inspection. Check displays, especially the more interactive ones where resources may need replacing or tidying. If you've got a geography display up in the school and you see an inspector hovering nearby, don't be afraid to go and explain more about it. They'll probably be interested and if they really do have to be going somewhere they are sure to tell you in a tactful way! It's likely that your positive approach and enthusiasm will have been noted.

Keep in close touch with other subject coordinators, share information about interviews with inspectors and support each other where you can. For instance, when checking the geography resources you may see that some historical artefacts need tidying: have a word with the history coordinator.

During your subject interview be enthusiastic, concise and accurate in what you say. Comments are easily cross-checked so there's no point in stretching reality! Stress what is going well in geography. Show you are aware of what developments are needed and explain how and when you are planning to do these. Have some materials with you at the interview to support and illustrate your comments — your portfolio, some photographs of your contrasting locality, the new large scale local maps you've only just received, the assignment you did on a geography INSET course can all be helpful.

After the inspection

At the end of the inspection an oral feedback session must be held. The school should point out any factual errors. The headteacher is able to invite any member of staff whom they wish to attend. This is your chance to ensure that any errors of fact are made clear.

The geography paragraph in the final report will be of particular interest to you. Be encouraged by the positive findings and take note of anything that needs attention. The governing body has to draw up an action plan within forty working days of receiving the report. You may be involved in work leading up to this even though it may not directly involve geography. For instance, if issues arise about partnership with parents and community, you may be able to offer suggestions for developing these within the geography curriculum.

In some schools the report may be the opportunity to get initiatives under way which have received resistance in the past. The quality of learning resources may be criticised. You need to be ready to respond with ideas about what will be needed for geography.

In the light of the report you may need to adjust your action plan. This is best done as a whole school activity to help achieve a coordinated approach. Hopefully, the inspection will have been a positive experience and one on which you may build your role as geography coordinator.

Part five   Resources for learning

Chapter 13   Gaining, maintaining and deploying resources

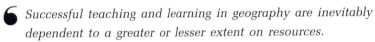
Successful teaching and learning in geography are inevitably dependent to a greater or lesser extent on resources.

(Palmer, 1994)

One of your jobs as geography coordinator will be the management of the subject resources. It's a never ending task because items need replacing, curriculum developments occur and new materials are always temptingly appearing. In reality you will probably have a small budget. Part of your success in effectively resourcing geography will therefore depend on how well you prioritise purchases and your ability to obtain items for little or no cost.

Your first task is to make a list of all the geography resources you can find in the school. Some may be worn out, stereotyped or out-of-date — get rid of these now. It will save doing it just before your inspection! A few good quality materials are better than many poor ones. This will not be a problem with general stock stored centrally, but you may have more of a problem if in the past teachers have been able to choose and buy materials which have then become part of 'their' classroom stock. If this is a serious problem it is a good idea to talk to the headteacher. S/he may be able to help in either disposing of these resources or arranging for them to be stored in a more effective way.

When you know what is available, look at your schemes of work and decide what resources are needed to teach each part. If your planning documents have a 'resources' heading you may be able to identify what is used, or at least intended to be used, in the various units of work. There could be two decisions to make. One might be to decide on a list of resources which can be used across the curriculum; for instance, compasses and a range of globes. Your list of these may indicate what needs to be stored centrally with easy access for teachers and, in some cases, children. The second decision will be based on items needed for particular units of work. These might include a commercially produced pack for studying a distant locality, photographs of your school locality and maps needed for your residential field visit.

Only you will be able to decide on priorities in your school. Talk to colleagues and find out what they think is useful, which may also tell you something about their approach to geography. It is important to make this selection process as transparent as possible otherwise you may alienate some staff who feel their year group is being treated unfairly. Discuss ideas at a staff meeting so at least everyone knows why decisions have been taken.

You can base your priorities on a number of things:

What parts of the geography curriculum urgently need some basic resources?

Are there any special projects you want to get off the ground e.g. a new residential visit?

Is it this year that the PTA will be providing money for special purchases of major items? A range of globes, inflatable globes and satellite images might be on your shopping list for them.

There may be a severe lack of any maps and plans for locality studies. These could be an essential first stage in resource development.

These buying decisions will then become part of the development plan for geography. Use this list and plan in discussions with the headteacher, because you are likely to have to make your case just as other coordinators will be doing.

Where can money come from to buy resources?

Here are some case studies collected by the author to show what can be done by an imaginative approach to resourcing geography:

Commercially produced aerial photographs of your school locality can be expensive. One school put out a request in a parents' newsletter asking if anyone had contacts with private pilots. One was quickly found. A discussion was held about the types of oblique and vertical photographs that would be relevant. For the cost of two rolls of film, processing and laminating, the school then had a set of very flexible and up-to-date resources. The content was relevant to pupils because they could relate to many of the features and extend their learning from them. A particular benefit was that groups of photos were taken at different altitudes. This was a most useful resource to begin looking at issues of scale.

Another school was working hard to develop links with other European schools to enhance their thematic studies at Key Stage 2, but could not afford a fax machine. The headteacher was friendly with the local garage with a fax machine next to the school. She struck a deal by which the only costs to the school were the phone calls. This facility was very successful. Everyone could see its relevance to geography and English work and now the school links across Europe every day via e-mail. It's recently won a national competition for its web pages.

An infant school headteacher keeps an ear to the ground about where her staff are going on holiday. She has worked with them on the types of artefacts which help young children begin to learn about the wider world. Friendly reminders encourage them to bring something back from each visit. The school now has an excellent range of resources for teachers to draw on. Items particularly relating to children such as reading books in other languages, toys and games help pupils to relate to the lives of children in other countries. Each item on its own is cheap but together they make up a priceless teaching resource for geography. In the same school, pupils are encouraged to send a postcard to the school when they go on holiday. The postcard collection is building up into an interesting and flexible resource.

- the school budget;
- PTA and friends of the school;
- special funds available from the LEA (often set up for particular curriculum development — keep alert and enquire about these);
- local industry and commerce;
- local, regional and national competitions related to environmental issues for example;
- funding from the European Union for European initiatives.

None of these will offer fortunes but each success provides something which would otherwise not be in your school.

The nature of geography does mean that some relevant and high quality resources can be entirely free, apart perhaps from some phone calls and leg-work on your part. Try to develop some skills in lateral thinking to find the right sources, but the real skill lays in searching out possibilities and being alert to opportunities and links you can make. One technique is to think about what you are looking for and then try to identify people and organisations beyond the school who also use those things. For instance, I was preparing an INSET day in a Cotswold town and needed to get some maps copied, so I went to the local printers. It was clear the owner was interested in the range of old maps and after some discussion a fascinating set of drawings appeared showing both sides of the high street in the 1940s. It transpired that they had been drawn by an artist who could not pay his hotel bill and the printer's father had owned the hotel. These prints, hidden away in a drawer for years, formed the basis of a fascinating local enquiry about how the town had and was still changing. The printer also introduced me to other most helpful people in the town.

Making and collecting resources to which the children can relate is another part of your role. As in all subjects, many commercially produced and relatively expensive materials are available, but few of them will relate to your locality and other places you will study. It is often far better to spend money on resources which will be relevent to your needs. These include sets of local photographs, a range of maps and plans and locally produced materials relating to your units of

These examples of resourcing are given to help you focus on the opportunities which may exist in your school:

The sand tray in the infants is excellent for model making.

- Can teachers prepare activities for children to make islands and special landscapes? Can they provide flags with words such as 'bay', 'beach' and 'hill' for the children to place on their finished model?

The programmable robot normally used for maths can become a taxi for which the children design a route to collect teddy bear passengers from around the classroom.

A model farm can introduce children to ideas about landuse if structured activites are designed by the teacher. They can then put the finished farm on the floor and look down on it from an aerial view. Some could then try to draw this view as a part of the process in moving away from the 3-D world to the 2-D abstract version we see in maps.

work. Textbooks concentrating on isolated geography skills and sets of photocopiable worksheets rarely provide the levels of relevance and continuity needed to build a set of worthwhile and practical learning experiences.

There are a few exceptions to this. You may well need to buy commercially produced resources for the study of a distant locality outside the UK. A range of non-fiction reference books on other countries and issues such as rainforests and weather will also be needed, but books are expensive and date quickly so investigate the extent to which the school library service can help and how much the staff find this of use.

There are probably many resources in your school which are not labelled 'geography' yet they may make excellent geography resources. Being aware of these helps to keep expenses down while covering aspects of the Orders in your work. Part of your role is to help colleagues identify the possibilities and demonstrate how activities can be prepared which teach important aspects of geography.

Looking for such opportunities and actually trying out some of the ideas can form the basis of an interesting and practical staff development session.

In the research chapter we saw some evidence for the considerable time coordinators spend in managing resources. Activites such as cataloguing new materials, keeping resources tidy, repairing equipment and making new items all take time. They are important jobs because staff may be more inclined to use resources which are easy to find and do the job for which they were intended. Try to set a time for checking the state of the geography resources on a regular basis. In that way the job should never get out of control. Ideally, you may be able to arrange for some help, perhaps from a parent or classroom assistant: your valuable expertise and time is probably better spent working alongside colleagues rather than laminating thirty photographs.

At some stage you will need to look at how resources are stored, catalogued and accessed in your school. Storage is partly a matter of policy. If you are working towards an environment in which teachers have the skills and confidence to regularly build geography into classroom life, they will need easy access to resources. This may require that each class or year group has a globe, wall maps and a few carefully chosen atlases. Teachers will then know that they can, for example, easily have a brief discussion about a world event and use resources which are close at hand.

People will use resources if they are readily available. You could, for example, build up sets of plans of the school buildings, grounds, locality and region which are duplicated and centrally stored in a filing cabinet. If you regularly make sure there is always a supply available, staff will draw on this resource. They will appreciate the fact that they do not have to make their own copies each time they want to use them. Incidentally, this would also have the effect of you being able to keep some control over the quality of resources given to children.

While some basic resources do need to be kept in classrooms, many will be centrally stored. This prevents costly duplication and can make it a little easier for you to maintain them. The first stage of this process is to discuss with the headteacher where the storage area will be sited. If your school has a clear and effective policy for children and staff having access to resources as an essential feature of an effective learning environment, you may decide to keep everything in the library or resource base. If this is not practical for security or other reasons, try to find somewhere which will keep geography's profile at a high level. An small, easily accessible and visible location in the staffroom is better than a cupboard at the far end of the school, even if it is bigger!

Prepare a list of resources which clearly explains where things are kept. Give a copy to everyone on the staff. Keep it up to date. This can be helpful in a number of ways. For instance, it is not necessary to buy large sets of atlases. It is far better to have a few with various levels of details and content. If they are based in certain classrooms and teachers know where they can be found, they may make more use of them and plan differentiated activites because they know they can get hold of a range of materials.

There are some things which you need to keep well away from the dangers of school life. This approach can save you a great deal of time and money in the long run! Here are some examples of how a little time and planning can make your life a lot easier. All of them come from real examples seen in schools:

Your orienteering compasses come complete with a useful instruction book. Copy the book. Put the copy out with the compasses and keep the original. When the copy gets lost or covered in mud, you can still make another copy.

Don't leave the negatives of your locality photographs in the same photo wallet that goes into classrooms. Keep them with your own resources. This stops them from disappearing without trace.

If the video of your river study is going to get a lot of use, make a copy for classroom use and keep the original safe.

If you have old maps, make copies after taking advice from your LEA staff on what copyright contracts operate in your county. There will be some wonderful examples which you want children to see and use in their original form. Spend some time deciding how they can best be protected and get this done.

Liaise with the IT coordinator to have copies made within the copyright agreement of any geography software and related documents. Keep originals away from classrooms at all times!

It can be a good idea to keep a record of where various items came from in case you do need to replace anything. Start a list of contacts, names and addresses and suppliers of geography resources.

As new items arrive for the collection of geography resources you will be keen for staff to use them at appropriate times. They will need to know they exist and may like ideas on how to use them. This can be done formally during staff meetings and development sessions. It can also be done less formally but often as effectively, by some carefully planned publicity. Perhaps you have just bought a set of satellite images — can you arrange a simple active display in a prominent part of the school? Ask the headteacher if they are planning an assembly story and discussion based around another country as they might be able to use the images during the assembly.

You will probably find it frustrating not being able to have all the resources you know would make geography a much richer subject in your school. You will be doing a good job if you establish your priorities, spend your budget carefully and know how to get useful resources at no cost. Keep everything in order and help teachers to make the most of what you do have. Build a vision of where you would like to get to and work steadily towards it.

Chapter 14   Resources for primary geography

> ❝ The most important but not the only resource for geographical work is the local area.
>
> (Catling, 1993)

Lists of book titles, atlases and videos date very quickly so instead, this chapter lists the range of resources which will help children have a variety of interesting and relevant geographical experiences covering the Orders and hopefully beyond. You will probably not be able to afford to have everything in your school, therefore the list is designed to help you plan, prioritise and select those items which will be most appropriate for your school. Ideas are also included to guide you towards the location of suitable resources.

When you need specific addresses and contact points you can use a number of sources:

■ Geography resources are regularly reviewed in *Primary Geographer* published by the Geographical Association. It often contains articles relating to geographical resources;

■ One of the largest and most up to date exhibition of resources will be found each year at the Geographical Association's Annual Conference. This is held during the Easter holiday at different venues around the country each year;

■ LEA advisers and centres keep information about what is available;

- *The Times Educational Supplement* contains resource reviews and the occasional Geography supplements give even more details;

- Professional journals such as *Child Education* often review resources;

- University Departments of Education and training colleges aim to keep an up to date selection of resources across the primary subjects;

- Many organisations keep information on resources and suppliers related to their area of interest. Urban studies and Development Education Centres are examples;

- County Council planning offices, tourist information offices and local studies centres in libraries are excellent starting points for collecting local maps, plans, photographs etc.

- More and more information is becoming available on the web. Use this if you have access;

- Keep in touch with other geography coordinators and share ideas. They will have tried things out and know if they work;

- Be aware of non-educational sources. For example, the local environmental group can probably help with your locality studies.

The following alphabetical list could be used as a checklist when you are auditing your resources and later as something to refer back to when checking on your progress. The sources printed above will give you details of publishers and suppliers at the times you are getting them. Details change so quickly that a list in this book would date within weeks of printing.

Aerial photographs

It is essential to have these for your school locality and ideally for other places, as you can afford them. A range of scales is useful. LEAs often have special contracts for supplying them. Vertical and oblique photographs should be in your collection.

Artefacts

Toys, books, stamps, foods, hats and games from around the world are just a few of the things you can begin to collect.

Atlases

These are expensive and date very quickly. Instead of buying class sets, buy perhaps six each of a wide selection to cover a variety of age /ability ranges and types of content. Bradley and Moore (1992) provide a very useful discussion of the criteria you can use when choosing atlases.

Big books and atlases

Various publishers produce these for the early years. Some are excellent, stimulating resources for younger children.

Cassettes and compact discs

A collection of music from around the world can add much to geographical studies.

Central Bureau for Education Visits and Exchanges

Contact them for information and advice on European links, funding and study visits.

Central Bureau for Educational Visits and Exchanges
10 Spring Gardens
London
SW1A 2BN

0171 389 4004

Children's literature

Many children's books can be used to develop geographical ideas and are probably already in your school library. A regular feature in *Primary Geographer* gives many ideas for using them in the classroom. Look out for sections in books for adults, for instance, *Heart of Darkness* by Joseph Conrad provides superb images of an African river.

Compasses and orienteering equipment

These can be used in a wide range of fieldwork situations and are a valuable resources for teaching mapping skills.

Contrasting localities

While you can buy commercial packs, the best results come from working with another school in your contrasting UK locality, in Europe and the wider world. Your exchange of letters, e-mails, videos, photos, maps, artefacts and even Christmas cakes will be the most up to date, interesting and challenging resources you can use for any contrasting locality study. Halocha (1997c) suggests ways of starting this with photographs and maps.

Computer software

Information technology should be planned into geography where relevant. Keep up to date with software publications and try them before you buy. Many do not live up to expectations. Liaise with the IT coordinator in your school. Plan to develop a range to include data handling, simulations, obtaining information about people, places and environments and helping children to understand the impact of IT on the changing world.

CD-ROMs

Part of the above section really, but highlighted as they can provide access to the wider world and help pupils develop enquiry skills if activities are carefully planned. CD-ROM atlases, simulations and information databases can all be valuable.

E-mail

This is an excellent resource for developing links with your other localities. If your school has e-mail talk to colleagues about how it might be used. Sending and receiving messages connected with geographical enquiry is a relevant means of developing many requirements of the English Orders.

Field study centres

Find out what your LEA can still offer in terms of local centres and those further afield. Private organisations also provide centres and specialist courses. Plan how these resources will be integrated within your whole school geography plans.

Fieldwork equipment

This will vary according to what your chosen study areas offer for enquiry. Fieldwork is an essential part of geographical studies and this equipment will probably be high on your buying list. Clipboards, relevant maps and plans, clinometers, camera, film etc. will need to be budgeted for. See what is already available around the school before spending your budget.

Geographical Association

This is one of your main resources and form of support and you can press hard for the school to become a member. You will probably want to become a personal member too. Regular contact with geography through the GA will keep you up to date and fully informed on all key developments and ideas for teaching primary geography. The association provides:

- Four editions a year of *Primary Geographer* to all members;
- Four newsletters a year;
- An annual conference with free admission to everyone interested in geography: this includes the biggest exhibition of geography resources in the country, lectures, workshops and seminars and field visits;

- Books, teaching packs and leaflets on a wide range of practical teaching issues;
- An annual primary conference;
- Regional and local branch activities;
- Grants for research and travel;
- They would also be very interested to receive articles from you for *Primary Geographer* discussing geographical activities you have found to be successful.

Contact them at:

The Geographical Association
160 Solly Street
Sheffield
S1 4BF
telephone: 0114 296 0088
fax:　　　 0114 296 7176

Globes

Try to build up a range of these: standard globes both physical and political, large inflatable globes, write-on globes, historical globes. Catling (1996b) offers a range of interesting ways of using these in the classroom.

Information technology

This can include many things for geography. Programmable robots, data loggers, ceefax, world wide web, Metfax, are just a few examples.

Local Agenda 21

If this is active in your area, it will be an excellent starting point for resources and issues in environmental education which are to be studied at Key Stages 1 and 2.

Locality

This is perhaps your main geography resource. Platten (1992) provides many suggestions for identifying local resources: buildings, transport systems, workplaces, the physical landscape, the people, the climate, and environmental issues will all offer the basic and essential resources you need for effective geography teaching.

Local community

School governors, parents, local industry, commerce and other organisations can all be excellent resources. Decide which ones might be worth investigating and set off!

Locality packs

If you don't use direct links with other localities, some carefully selected locality packs can be used as a starting point. They will need to be supplemented with other resources such as satellite images, reference books and perhaps linked television programmes.

Maps and plans

A range of local maps and plans are essential. Foley and Janikoun (1996) list many you can collect free in your locality. Catling (1988) explains in detail the range of scales and content needed at Key Stages 1 and 2. It is important to build up a wide selection of local maps and plans starting with a plan of the school, its grounds, the streets around and the wider locality. Old maps can also be added to show how the locality is constantly changing. Look out for a wide variety of maps and plans and begin to build up a school resource box of them, for example, London Underground, supermarket floor plans, architect's plans, tourist leaflets.

Models

Your collection of these will grow as they are made by pupils and might include a model of your village, a volcano etc. A sand tray for simulating river processes is an excellent resource to make and have available. Asquith, Chambers and Donert (1996) provide many ideas on making and using practical resources for river studies.

Photographs

Your collection of these will be built up as you develop your studies in all the localities. Have them printed as large as the school can afford. Laminate and number them. A description of what they show and the date the photo was taken are very useful, especially when they become school history resources in a few years' time!

Playmats

Great Britain, Europe and the world as well as farms, town streets and others are all useful.

Radio

Programmes such as *In the News* (BBC radio) can be used in geographical studies.

Reference books

A range of books on people and places around the world and aspects of geography such as rivers, homes, environmental issues, the weather, rocks etc. will need to be developed. This is a huge task so begin by looking closely at the needs of your units of study.

Rock, soil and fossil samples

Share this work with the science coordinator as you both have overlapping areas of interest. A collection of rocks, soils and fossils from your locality make a good starting point. Make contact with the local quarry manager and monumental stonemasons.

Satellite images

Superb images are now available. Your LEA adviser and adverts in *Primary Geographer* will guide you to the latest available sources. Try to include one showing your local area and then cover the UK, Europe and the world as you can afford them.

School buildings and grounds

There are two ways of looking at school grounds as a resource. The first is to take them as they are and use them as part of your locality. The second is to deliberately build features into the school to enhance geographical work. Examples of these include north, south, east, west labels on classroom walls; an outline map of the world, compass points and a 10 × 10 square grid painted on the playground; a weathervane on a roof; labels on objects in infant classrooms; a senses trail around the school; a wildlife area. You will be able to think of many more. Look out for other ideas as you visit other schools.

Television

An excellent range of programmes is now broadcast to support geography at Key Stages 1 and 2. Support materials are often available and together with recordings of the programmes can be planned into units of work. Study the yearly BBC and ITV programme details and arrange to record the programmes you need.

Videos

Be selective. Commercial geographical videos rarely come up to the standard of schools' TV programmes. The most useful ones will probably be those you make as part of your enquiries and those exchanged with other localities. However, look for geographical opportunities in videos such as *The Snowman* which contain excellent sequences.

Wall charts

The world, Europe and Great Britain are starting points. Add others as you can afford them.

Weather recording equipment

Some of this can be bought and is probably already in your school. Many pieces of equipment can be made by the children themselves and provide excellent opportunities for work in technology. Discuss the possibilities with your school technology coordinator.

World Wide Web

This is rapidly becoming a useful resource. Information on natural events such as volcanoes etc. all bring the real world into the classroom.

References

ALEXANDER, R., ROSE, J. and WOODHEAD, C. (1992), *Curriculum Organisation and Classroom Practice in Primary Schools*, HMSO: London.

ALEXANDER, R., WILLCOCKS, J., KINDER, K. and NELSON, N. (1995), *Versions of Primary Education*, London: Routledge.

ASHCROFT, K. and PALACIO, D. (1997), *Implementing the Primary Curriculum. A Teacher's Guide*, London: Falmer Press.

ASQUITH, S., CHAMBERS, B. and DONERT, K. (1996), *Geography Curriculum Bank Key Stage 2: Themes*, Leamington Spa: Scholastic.

BELBIN, R.M. (1981), *Management Teams: Why they Succeed or Fail*, Oxford: Bulterwoolt-Heinemann.

BELL, D. (1997), *What do curriculum/subject co-ordinators in primary schools do?* Paper presented at the British Educational Research Association Conference, University of York, 1997.

BELL, B. and GILBERT, J. (1996), *Teacher Development: a Model from Science Education*, London: Falmer Press.

BLAND, K., CHAMBERS, W., DONERT, K. and THOMAS, A.D. (1996), 'Fieldwork in geography' in BAILEY, P. (ed) *Handbook for Geography Teachers*, Sheffield: The Geographical Association.

BOOTH, R., CHAMBERS, W.J. and THOMAS, A.D. (1993), *Reaching Out*, London: Living Earth/ICI.

BOWLES, R. (1995), 'How well do you know your locality?' *Primary Geographer*, **23**, Sheffield: Geographical Association.

BOWLES, R. (1996), 'Primary Geography Research Register', *Primary Geographer*, **27**.

BRADLEY, L. and MOORE, J. (1992), 'A Review of Atlases for Key Stages 1 and 2', *Primary Geographer*, **11**, Sheffield: Geographical Association.

BUTT, G., LAMBERT, D. and TELFER, S. (1995), *Assessment Works. Approaches to assessment in geography at Key Stages 1, 2 and 3*, Sheffield: Geographical Association.

CATLING, S. (1988), 'Maps and mapping', *Geographical Work in Primary and Middle Schools*, Sheffield: Geographical Association.

CATLING, S. (1993), 'Co-ordinating Geography', *Primary Geographer*, **14**, Sheffield: Geographical Association.

CATLING, S. (1995), 'Choosing and using places', *Primary Geographer*, **21**, Sheffield: Geographical Association.

CATLING, S. (1996a), *Placing Places*, Sheffield: The Geographical Association.

CATLING, S. (1996b), 'Beginning to map the world. Introducing the world map to 4–7 year-olds', *Primary Geographer*, **24**, Sheffield: Geographical Association.

CCW (1991), *Geography in the National Curriculum: Non-Statutory Guidance for Teachers*, Cardiff: Welsh Office.

CHAMBERS, B. and DONERT, K. (1996), *Teaching Geography at Key Stage 2*, Cambridge: Chris Kington.

DARVIZEH, Z. and SPENCER, C.P. (1984), 'How do young children learn novel routes? The importance of landmarks in the child's retracing of routes through the large scale environment', *Environmental Education and Information*, **3**, pp. 97–105.

DAY, C., HALL, C., GAMMAGE, P. and COLES, M. (1993), *Leadership and the Curriculum in the Primary School*, London: PCP.

DEARING, R. (1993), *The National Curriculum and its Assessment*, London: SCAA.

DES (1989), *Aspects of Education: The teaching and learning of history and geography*, London: DES.

DES (1990), *Geography for Ages 5–16: Proposals of the Secretary of State for Education and Science and the Secretary of State for Wales*, London: HMSO.

DfE (1995), *Key Stages 1 and 2 of the National Curriculum*, London: DfE.

EVERARD, K.B. and MORRIS, G. (1985), *Effective School Management*, London: PCP.

FOLEY, M. and JANIKOUN, J. (1996), *The Really Practical Guide to Primary Geography*, London: Stanley Thornes.

GEOGRAPHICAL ASSOCIATION/NATIONAL COUNCIL FOR EDUCATION TECHNOLOGY (1995), *Primary Geography: A Pupil's Entitlement to IT*, Sheffield: Geographical Association.

GIPPS, C. (1994), *Beyond Testing: Towards a Theory of Educational Assessment*, London: Falmer Press.

GONZALEZ, B. and GONZALEZ, E. (1997), 'Equal Opportunities and the Teaching of Geography' in TILBURY, D. and WILLIAMS, M. *Teaching and Learning Geography*, London: Routledge.

GRAVES, N. (1997), 'Geographical education in the 1990s' in TILBURY, D. and WILLIAMS, M. (eds) *Teaching and Learning Geography*, London: Routledge.

HALOCHA, J. (1997a), 'The European Dimension in Primary Education' in TILBURY, D. and WILLIAMS, M. *Teaching and Learning Geography*, London: Routledge.

HALOCHA, J. (1997b), *Opening doors — opening minds: Developing a European perspective with Primary Children and their Teachers*, Paper presented at the British Educational Research Association Conference, University of York, 1997.

HALOCHA, J. (1997c), 'Focus on your locality' *Primary Geographer*, **29**, Sheffield: Geographical Association.

HARRIS, C. (1996), 'Managing, and benefiting from, an OFSTED inspection' in BAILEY, P. and FOX, P. *Geography Teachers' Handbook*, Sheffield: Geographical Association.

HARRISON, M. (1995), *Developing a leadership role in Key Stage 2 Curriculum*, London: Falmer Press.

HARRISON, M. (1998), *Coordinating IT across the Primary School*, London: Falmer Press.

HICKS, D. (1994), *Educating for the future: A practical classroom guide*, London: World Wide Fund for Nature.

HILLMAN, M. (1998), in SCOFFHAM, S. (ed) *Researching Primary Geography*, Sheffield: Geographical Association.

HMSO (1989) *Aspects of Primary Education: The Teaching and Learning of History and Geography*, London: DES.

HMSO (1995), *The OFSTED Handbook. Guidance on the Inspection of Nursery and Primary Schools*, London: HMSO.

KIMBER, D., CLOUGH, N., FORREST, M., HARNETT, P., MENTER, L. and NEWMAN, E. (1995), *Humanities in Primary Education*, London: David Fulton.

LEWIS, L. (1996), 'Inside story', *Primary Geographer*, **27**, Sheffield: Geographical Association.

MACKINTOSH, M. (1997), *Is there a place for a constructivist approach in primary geography — or have we missed the opportunity?* Paper presented at the Charney Manor Primary Geography Conference, March 1997.

MARSDEN, B. (1994), 'Beyond locational knowledge: Good assesment practice in primary geography', in MARSDEN, B. and HUGHES, J. (eds) *Primary School Geography*, London: David Fulton.

MARTIN, F. (1995), *Teaching Early Years Geography*, Cambridge: Chris Kington.

MATTHEWS, M. (1992), *Making Sense of Place*, Lewes: Harvester-Wheatsheaf, Barnes & Noble.

MAY, S., RICHARDSON, P. and BANKS, V. (1993), *Fieldwork in Action 1: Planning Fieldwork*, Sheffield: The Geographical Association.

MAY, S. and COOK, J. (1993), *Fieldwork in Action 2: An Enquiry Approach*, Sheffield: The Geographical Association.

MAY, S. and THOMAS, T. (1994), *Fieldwork in Action 3: Managing Out-of-Classroom Activities*, Sheffield: The Geographical Association.

MAY, S. (1996), *Fieldwork in Action 4: Primary Fieldwork Projects*, Sheffield: The Geographical Association.

MCGARRIGLE, J. and DONALDSON, M. (1974), 'Conservation Accidents', *Cognition*, **3**, pp. 341–50.

MEE, K. (1996), 'Assessment: new opportunities', *Primary Geographer*, **24**, Sheffield: Geographical Association.

MORGAN, W. (1994), 'Making a place for geography: The Geographical Association's initiatives and the Geography

Working Group's Experience' in MARSDEN, B. and HUGHES, J. *Primary School Geography*, London: David Fulton.

MORGAN, W. (1995), *Plans for Primary Geography*, Sheffield: The Geographical Association.

NAISH, M. (1997), 'The scope of school geography: a medium for education' in TILBURY, D. and WILLIAMS, M. (eds) *Teaching and Learning Geography*, London: Routledge.

NATIONAL CURRICULUM COUNCIL (1990), *Curriculum Guidance 7 Environmental Education*, York: NCC.

NATIONAL CURRICULUM COUNCIL (1993), *Teaching Geography at Key Stages 1 and 2: An INSET Guide*, York: NCC.

OFFICE FOR STANDARDS IN EDUCATION (OFSTED) (1994a), *Primary Matters: A Discussion on Teaching and Learning in Primary Schools*, London: OFSTED.

OFFICE FOR STANDARDS IN EDUCATION (OFSTED) (1995b), *Guidance on the Inspection of Nursery and Primary Schools*, London: HMSO.

OFFICE FOR STANDARDS IN EDUCATION (OFSTED) (1995c), *Geography: A Review of Inspection Findings 1993/94*, London: HMSO.

PALMER, J. (1992), 'Life experiences of environmental educators', *Environmental Education*, Winter.

PALMER, J. (1993), 'From Santa Claus to sustainability: emergent understanding of concepts and issues in environmental science', *International Journal of Science Education*, **15**, 5, pp. 487–96.

PALMER, J. (1994), *Geography in the Early Years*, London: Routledge.

PIAGET, J. (1929), *The Child's Conception of the World*, London: Kegan Paul.

PIAGET, J. and INHELDER, B. (1956), *The Child's Conception of Space*, London: Routledge and Kegan Paul.

PIAGET, J. and WEIL, A-M. (1951), 'The development in children of the idea of the homeland and of relations with other countries', *Institute of Social Science Bulletin*, **3**, pp. 356–78.

PIGGOTT, B. (1995), 'Differentiation in Geography', *Primary Geographer*, **21**, Sheffield: The Geographical Association.

PLATTEN, L. (1992), 'Resourcing Local Studies', *Primary Geographer*, **11**, Sheffield: Geographical Association.

PLAYFOOT, D., SKELTON, M. and SOUTHWORTH, G. (1989), *The Primary School Management Book*, London: Mary Glasgow Publishers Ltd.

RANGER, G. (1995), 'A slimmer, trimmer geography — the rationale for curriculum change', *Primary Geographer*, **21**, Sheffield: Geographical Association.

RAWLINGS, E. (1992), *Programmes of Study: Try this Approach*, Sheffield: Geographical Association.

RICHARDSON, P. (1995), 'Inspecting Geography in the Primary School', *Primary Geographer*, **23**, Sheffield: Geographical Association.

RICHIE, R. (1997), *The subject co-ordinator's role and responsibilities in primary schools*, Paper presented to the British Educational Research Association Conference, University of York, 1997.

SCAA (1995a), *Geography. A review of inspection findings 1993/94*, London: HMSO.

SCAA (1995b), *Planning the curriculum at Key Stages 1 and 2*, London: SCAA.

SCAA (1996a), *Teaching Environmental Matters through the National Curriculum*, London: SCAA.

SCAA (1996b), *Planning the curriculum for pupils with profound and multiple learning difficulties*, London: SCAA.

SCAA (1997a), *Geography at Key Stage 2. Curriculum Planning Guidance for Teachers*, London: SCAA.

SCAA (1997b), *Expectations in Geography at Key Stages 1 and 2*, London: SCAA.

SCAA (1997c, Summer Term), *Geography Update*, London: SCAA.

SCAA (1997d), *Geography and the Use of Language*, London: SCAA.

SCAA (1997e), *Use of Language: A Common Approach*, London: SCAA.

SCAA (1997f), *Looking at Children's Learning*, London: SCAA.

SCOFFHAM, S. (ed) (1998), *Researching Primary Geography*, Sheffield: Geographical Association.

SEBBA, J. (1991), *Planning for Geography for Pupils with Learning Difficulties*, Sheffield: Geographical Association.

SEBBA, J. (1995), *Geography for all*, London: David Fulton.

SMITH, P. (1997), 'Differentiation: Some definitions and examples', *Primary Geographer*, **28**, Sheffield: Geographical Association.

SPENCER, C., BLADES, M. and MORSLEY, K. (1989), *The Child in the Physical Environment*, Chichester: John Wiley & Sons.

STORM, M. (1989), 'The five basic questions for primary geography', *Primary Geographer*, **2**, p. 4, Sheffield: Geographical Association.

SWEASEY, P. (1997) *Studying Contrasting Localities*, Sheffield: Geographical Association.

THRELFALL, M. (1997), 'Planning across the curriculum', in ASHCROFT, K. and PALACIO, D. *Implementing the Primary Curriculum. A Teacher's Guide*, London: Falmer Press.

VAN MANEN, M. (1977), 'Linking ways of knowing with ways of being practical' in *Curriculum Inquiry*, **6**, 3.

VYGOTSKY, L.S. (1979) *Minds and Society*, Cambridge, MA: Harvard University Press.

WALFORD, R. (1997), 'The Great Debate and 1988' in TILBURY, D. and WILLIAMS, M. (eds) *Teaching and Learning Geography*, London: Routledge.

WEBB, R. (1994), *After the deluge: Changing roles and responsibilities in the primary school*, London: ATL.

WEBB, R. and VULLIAMY, G. (1996), *Roles and Responsibilities in the Primary School*, Buckingham: Open University Press.

WIEGAND, P. (1992), *Places in the Primary School. Knowledge and Understanding of Places at Key Stages 1 and 2*, London: Falmer Press.

WIEGAND, P. (1993), *Children and Primary Geography*, London: Cassell.

WIEGAND, P. (1997), 'Assessment in the primary school', in TILBURY, D. and WILLIAMS, M. *Teaching and Learning Geography*, London: Routledge.

WIEGAND, P. (1998), 'Understanding the World' in SCOFFHAM, S. *Researching Primary Geography*, Sheffield: Geographical Association.

Index

ORDER FORM

Post: *Customer Services Department, Falmer Press, Rankine Road, Basingstoke, Hampshire, RG24 8PR*
Tel: *(01256) 813000* **Fax**: *(01256) 479438*
E-mail: *book.orders@tandf.co.uk*

**10% DISCOUNT AND FREE P&P FOR SCHOOLS OR INDIVIDUALS ORDERING THE COMPLETE SET
ORDER YOUR SET NOW. WITH CREDIT CARD PAYMENTS, YOU WON'T BE CHARGED TILL DESPATCH.**

TITLE	DUE	ISBN	PRICE	QTY
SUBJECT LEADERS' HANDBOOKS SET		**(RRP £207.20)**	**£185.00**	
Coordinating Science	2/98	0 7507 0688 0	£12.95	
Coordinating Design and Technology	2/98	0 7507 0689 9	£12.95	
Coordinating Maths	2/98	0 7507 0687 2	£12.95	
Coordinating Physical Education	2/98	0 7507 0693 7	£12.95	
Coordinating History	2/98	0 7507 0691 0	£12.95	
Coordinating Music	2/98	0 7507 0694 5	£12.95	
Coordinating Geography	2/98	0 7507 0692 9	£12.95	
Coordinating English at Key Stage 1	4/98	0 7507 0685 6	£12.95	
Coordinating English at Key Stage 2	4/98	0 7507 0686 4	£12.95	
Coordinating IT	4/98	0 7507 0690 2	£12.95	
Coordinating Art	4/98	0 7507 0695 3	£12.95	
Coordinating Religious Education	Late 98	0 7507 0613 9	£12.95	
Management Skills for SEN Coordinators	Late 98	0 7507 0697 X	£12.95	
Building a Whole School Assessment Policy	Late 98	0 7507 0698 8	£12.95	
Curriculum Coordinator and OFSTED Inspection	Late 98	0 7507 0699 6	£12.95	
Coordinating Curriculum in Smaller Primary School	Late 98	0 7507 0700 3	£12.95	

I wish to pay by:

☐ Cheque *(Pay Falmer Press)*
☐ Pro-forma invoice
☐ Credit Card *(Mastercard / Visa / AmEx)*

Please add p&p	
orders up to £25	*10%*
orders from £25 to £50	*5%*
orders over £50	*free*

Value of Books	
P&P*	
Total	

Card Number _____ Expiry Date _____
Signature _____
Name _____ Title/Position _____
School _____
Address _____
_____
Postcode _____ Country _____
Tel no. _____ Fax _____
E-mail _____

Ref: 1197BFSLAD

☐ If you do not wish to receive further promotional information from
the Taylor&Francis Group, please tick box.
All prices are correct at time of going to print but may change without notice